The Man from Mukinupin

DOROTHY HEWETT

Currency Press,

Sydney

First published in print in 1979
by Fremantle Arts Centre Press, Fremantle, WA.
This edition first published in 2011 by
by Currency Press Pty Ltd,
Gadigal Land, Suite 310, 46-56 Kippax St, Surry Hills NSW 2010, Australia
enquiries@currency.com.au
www.currency.com.au

Cataloguing-in-Publication data for this title is available from the National
Library of Australia.

Typeset by Emma Vine, Currency Press.
Cover design by Katy Wall, Currency Press.
Currency Press acknowledges the Traditional Owners of the Country on which
we live and work. We pay our respects to all Aboriginal and Torres Strait
Islander Elders, past and present.

Contents

For my sons Joe, Michael and Tom Flood who, like their mother, grew up in the West.

It's a country full of old men, with thumbscrews
on their hunger,
Their crosses leaning sideways in the scrub.
My cousins spit to windward, great noses blue
with moonlight,
Their shoulders propping up the Kunjin pub.
From Dorothy Hewett, 'Once I Rode with
Clancy',

Windmill Country

I would like to thank the Literature Board of the Australia Council for the grant that made this play possible

Dorothy Hewett

The Man from Mukinupin was first performed by the National Theatre Company at the Playhouse, Perth, on 31 August 1979 with the following cast:

JACK TUESDAY / HARRY TUESDAY	Richard Tulloch
POLLY PERKINS / TOUCH OF THE TAR	Noni Hazlehurst
MISS CLARRY HUMMER / THE WIDOW TUESDAY	Margaret Ford
MISS CLEMMY HUMMER	Rosemary Barr
EDIE PERKINS	Sally Sander
EEK PERKINS / ZEEK PERKINS	Maurie Ogden
MERCY MONTEBELLO	Jenny McNae
CECIL BRUNNER / MAX MONTEBELLO / THE FLASHER	Bill Kerr

Directed by Stephen Barry
Designed by Tony Tripp
Music by Jim Cotter
Choreography by Jenny McNae
Lighting by Duncan Ord

CHARACTERS

JACK TUESDAY, the grocer's boy who becomes a J.C. Williamson's chorus boy; doubled with

HARRY TUESDAY, his twin brother, the shearer who becomes a shell-shocked war hero

POLLY PERKINS, the town beauty, Jack's sweetheart and the storekeeper's daughter; doubled with

LILY PERKINS, known as TOUCH OF THE TAR, Harry's sweetheart and the half-caste half-sister of Polly

MISS CLARRY HUMMER, the ex-wardrobe mistress of J.C. Williamson's, now the town dressmaker; doubled with

THE WIDOW TUESDAY, Jack and Harry's mother: a Dickensian lady

MISS CLEMMY HUMMER, ex-tightrope walker from Wirth's Circus, now mistress of ceremonies for the night people

EDIE PERKINS, Polly's deaf mother, a reciter of ballads

EEK PERKINS, Mukinupin storekeeper and Polly's father; doubled with

ZEEK PERKINS, his twin brother, a water diviner and stargazer

MERCY MONTEBELLO, an ageing Shakespearean actress, who marries Cecil Brunner

CECIL BRUNNER, travelling salesman in manchester goods and lingerie; doubled with

MAX MONTEBELLO, Italian actor/manager; and

THE FLASHER, town flasher and madman

SETTING

The action takes place in Mukinupin, a typical West Australian wheatbelt town east of the rabbit-proof fence. The time is 1912 to 1920.

Two unravelling wicker chairs are placed around a small table down right for the Misses Hummer, presenters of the play. Downstage left is the Perkins' General Store, with a counter and stools. Closer to centre stage is a cardboard pillared portico: the Mukinupin Town Hall. In Act Two this is inscribed with the legend 'Lest We Forget', and a cardboard war memorial of a soldier with a kelpie dog at his feet is placed upstage left of the Town Hall.

ACT ONE

In darkness the weird night music begins on the soundtrack, continuing until the mood of night and eeriness has been well set. The music is interspersed with a line of dialogue, an occasional giggle, scream, shout of laughter or a coo-ee.

ZEEK'S VOICE: [*chanting*] Water... Water... Water...

WIDOW TUESDAY'S VOICE: [*chanting*] Moth and rust... Rust and moth...

TOUCH OF THE TAR'S VOICE: [*calling*] Coo-ee... Coo-ee... [*a high giggle*].

HARRY TUESDAY'S VOICE: [*calling imperiously*] Lily! Lily Perkins!

TOUCH OF THE TAR'S VOICE: [*mocking, fading out*] Harr-ee! Harr-ee! Harr-ee!

EDIE PERKINS' VOICE: [*moaning*] Wash your hands... Put on your nightgown... Don't look so pale.

The background music rises to crescendo as, against the back scrim palely lit, and back to audience, is spread-eagled the shadow of THE FLASHER *in raincoat and felt hat, flashing.*

FLASHER: Look Polly! Look Polly! Look Polly!

Wild laughter, a scream, blackout.

ZEEK'S VOICE: [*continuing and growing in volume*] Water... Water... Water...

ZEEK'S VOICE *is broken by the sound of* CLEMMY HUMMER *knocking onstage with her crutch. Pause, silence. The church bells begin ringing and in dim blue light we see* CLEMMY *standing, back to audience, leaning on her crutch, downstage right, like a mistress of ceremonies. Enter the dancers,* ZEEK, HARRY, TOUCH OF THE TAR, *and* WIDOW TUESDAY, *all absolutely unrecognisable in their roles as rustic clog dancers. They are each carrying pitchforks and are dressed in gumboots, and wheat sheaves, so that they look like moving haystacks. They dance and sing the 'The Five Man's Morris' in a circle, with* CLEMMY *joining in as a kind of hobbling doppelganger.*

'THE FIVE MAN'S MORRIS'

ALL: We'll dance the five man's morris
We'll cart the sheaves away
We'll dance the Five Man's Morris
On Polly's wedding day.

We'll stook it and we'll fork it
We'll cease our labours soon
When the haystacks rise like magic
And we've stacked them to the moon.

Chorus:

Bringin' in the sheaves, bringin' in the sheaves
We'll bless all Mukinupin, bringin' in the sheaves.

The bells will toll and gold will roll
Around us in a ring
We'll bless all Mukinupin
When we bring the harvest in.

We'll dance the Five Man's Morris
We'll hear the teams roll by
When the evening star has vanished
And the Cross hangs in the sky.

Chorus:

Bringin' in the sheaves, bringin' in the sheaves
We'll bless all Mukinupin, bringin' in the sheaves.

Exit the dancers as CLEMMY HUMMER *turns downstage.*

CLEMMY: Goodnight Zeek, goodnight Flasher, goodnight Harry Tuesday, goodnight Lily Perkins, goodnight Widow Tuesday…

Her voice dies away with weariness, she yawns, the faint light of morning steals over the stage, a rooster crows, a magpie carols, as she hobbles to one of the two unravelling wicker chairs set beside a small table downstage right. She seats herself painfully, with the aid of her crutch, and relaxes, closing her eyes. As the stage lightens we can see backstage, up right, a cardboard pillared portico with 'MUKINUPIN TOWN HALL, 1912' in gold lettering. Downstage left is the Perkins' General Store with clothesline far left. Enter CLARRY HUMMER *carrying a silver tea tray set with coffeepot, sugar bowl, two coffee cups, a jug of cream on a doily. Both the* MISSES HUMMER *are smartly, brightly, and theatrically dressed from a bygone age:* MISS CLEMMY *a trifle askew, and on the edge of eccentricity.*

CLARRY: [*brightly*] Six a.m., Clem.

CLEMMY *wakes with a start, yawns, goes into their routine.*

CLEMMY: First light.

CLARRY *has set down the tray and herself, and is beginning to pour the coffee.*

CLARRY: The alarum clocks are ringing.

CLEMMY: Across the salt lakes.

CLARRY: East of the rabbit-proof fence.

They giggle. CLARRY *hands* CLEMMY *her coffee. They sit sipping.*

CLEMMY: Feels like another scorcher.

CLARRY: Dust in summer.

CLEMMY: Mud in winter.

CLARRY & CLEMMY: That's Mucka.

They laugh delightedly at their little routine. The town hall clock strikes six. CLARRY *checks it against her pocket watch fastened to her waist.*

CLARRY: Town Hall clock's on time.

Enter EEK PERKINS, *dressed in a conservative business suit and hat, checking his pocket watch. He takes up position in front of the scrim, shakes his watch and holds it to his ear.*

Eek Perkins is checking his watch.

CLEMMY: [*giggling*] Like the white rabbit.

CLARRY: Time's stopped.

CLEMMY: But he doesn't know it.

CLARRY: Doesn't know much, really.

CLEMMY: Profit and Loss.

CLARRY: Just a Mukinupin boy.

CLEMMY: Knows how to get on.

CLARRY: Get on what?

CLEMMY: [*in a stage whisper*] Gin jockey, they call him.

CLARRY pretends to be shocked, but giggles.

CLARRY & CLEMMY: No rain about, Mr P?

EEK: [*mournfully*] Not a cloud in the sky, Miss Clarry, Miss Clem.

They all shake their heads.

ALL: So bad for the crops.

EDIE: [*off, reciting, coming closer*]
> I sprang to the stirrup and Joris and he;
> I galloped, Dirck galloped, we galloped all three...

Enter EDIE PERKINS in smart beaded black: black bonnet trimmed with jet and carrying a huge ear trumpet. She joins EEK at the scrim still reciting.

> ... 'Good speed!' cried the watch,
> As the gate-bolts undrew...

EEK: [*loudly*] Mrs Perkins!

EDIE: ... 'Speed!' echoed the wall to us galloping through...

EEK: Edie Perkins!

EDIE: [*unaware*] ... Behind shut the postern, the lights sank to rest,
> And into the midnight we galloped abreast.

CLARRY: Edie Perkins, always was a good hand at a recitation.

CLEMMY: But amateur, hopelessly amateur.

CLARRY: And deaf as a post. Another cup, dear?

CLEMMY: Tone deaf. Please, dear.

EDIE: Eek Perkins, we'll never get there on time.

EEK: Get where, Mrs Perkins?

EDIE: [*loudly*] What's that?

She raises her ear trumpet

EEK: [*yelling*] Get where?

EDIE: Back to Mukinupin. Where's Polly? [*Agitated*] Where's my Polly?

POLLY: [*off*] I'm here, Mother.

Enter POLLY PERKINS, hair tied behind in a big bow, dressed in calf-length simple white muslin, white straw boater and smart button-up boots. She takes up position in front of the scrim.

EDIE: Ay?

> POLLY *kisses her cheek.*

POLLY: Here, Mother!

EEK: Are you coming with us, Polly?

POLLY: Where, Pa?

EEK: Back to Mukinupin before opening time.

POLLY: Why, Pa?

EEK: Polly, Polly Perkins, you're always asking questions.

POLLY: It's the only way to get any answers… isn't it?

> *Enter* JACK TUESDAY, *whistling* 'POLLY *Put the Kettle On'. He is dressed in black trousers, white shirtsleeves and a grocer's boy's white apron.*

JACK: Ask me a question, Pol?

POLLY: Do you love me, Jack?

JACK: More than all the tea in china.

> *Enter* CECIL BRUNNER *in shabby black with bowler hat, a sample case and a pink rosebud in his buttonhole.*

CECIL: Have an acid drop, Miss Polly?

POLLY Oh, thanks ever so, Mr Brunner.

> CECIL *removes an acid drop from his waistcoat pocket, gives it to* POLLY, *who dusts it, hesitates, pops it in her mouth.* JACK *grabs* POLLY *by the hand and twirls her into the set.*

JACK: Run faster, Polly, faster.

POLLY: Why? Why?

JACK: So Cecil Brunner can't ever catch you.

> *They laugh together, and whisper secrets.* CECIL *is stiff in front of the scrim.*

CECIL: I come to Mukinupin twice a year, travelling in manchester goods and… ladies' unmentionables.

> CECIL *crosses to the shop counter and raises his hat to the two* MISSES HUMMER.

Lovely weather, Miss Clarry, Miss Clem.

CLARRY & CLEMMY: Summer'll never end.

EDIE & EEK: No good for the crops.

They all nod their heads. EEK *picks up a roll of bunting, gestures to* JACK *to bring the ladder and goes out front of the shop. He holds the ladder while* JACK *climbs up with the bunting and fixes it above the shopfront. He hands* JACK *hammer and nails.* EDIE *crosses behind the counter and examines* CECIL*'s goods.*

EDIE: When the time comes, Mr Brunner will make our Pol a good husband.

She smiles benignly on CECIL.

POLLY: [*giggling*] With acid drops in his pocket.

EEK: Good, hard-working, sensible stamp of a chap.

POLLY: [*pouting*] Wears a corset and a toupée.

EDIE: Wears a Brunner rose in his buttonhole.

She leans forward to sniff at it.

EEK: Well-dressed, good family, not like young Jack.

EDIE: Who, Father?

EEK: Young Jack Tuesday.

EDIE *moves out towards the front of the shop.* JACK *climbs down the ladder, and the three of them admire the sign.* JACK *stuffs the hammer in his pocket.*

[*Reading proudly*] 'Perkins' General Store, 1912'.

EDIE: What was that, Mr Perkins? Speak up, Mr Perkins.

JACK *carries the ladder backstage.*

EEK: [*roaring*] Not like young Jack. [*Quietly*] Or his gaolbird twin brother, Harry.

EDIE: Not like your barmy twin brother, Zeek.

EEK: [*angrily*] Not much to choose between them.

EDIE: Eek and Zeek?

EEK: [*furiously*] Jack and Harry Tuesday… like as two peas.

EDIE: Eek and Zeek Perkins… identical twins!

POLLY: [*defiantly*] I love Jack Tuesday.

EEK: You'll love Cecil Brunner.

JACK: You love pink roses. I'll get you some.

JACK *begins to sweep the shop with the straw broom.* POLLY *unwinds her skipping rope, hands the two ends to* EEK *and* EDIE, *who turn rope for her.* CECIL *watches, smiling.*

POLLY: [*chanting*]
> Roses are pink, violets are blue,
> I've got a boyfriend and so have you.
> Tell your mother to hold her tongue,
> Tell your father to do the same,
> 'Cause he's the one who changed her name.
> Count the sheep going into the pen,
> Count them over and over again.

[*Skipping pepper*] Fifty, sixty, seventy, eighty, ninety, one hundred.

> *The rope turns faster and faster, till, breathless,* POLLY *gives up.* EEK *goes behind his counter and makes up his ledger.* EDIE *hangs the mat on the clothesline with* CECIL *'s help, and begins to beat it with the broom.* POLLY *takes her rope and skips slowly around the stage.* CLARRY *begins packing up the coffee things.* CLEMMY *takes a novel out from under the pillow.*

CLARRY: There's little Polly Perkins skipping down the street.

CLEMMY: Like the Queen of the May.

CLARRY: Growing up like a wildflower.

CLEMMY: There's Jack Tuesday sweeping out the Perkins' General Store.

CLARRY: He's sweet on Polly.

CLEMMY: That'll put the cat amongst the pigeons.

POLLY: [*pausing*] If I threw a bottle with a love letter in it into the middle of the salt-bush plain would anyone answer?

CLARRY: Course not—dead and buried.

CLEMMY: Under the sea.

EDIE: [*calling*] Get a move on, Polly, or I'll tan your BTM.

CLARRY: What's that you're reading, dear?

CLEMMY: [*wickedly whispering*] Passion in the Dust by Marie Corelli.

CLARRY: Oh! Clem! [*He crosses to exit with tray, smiling.*] Edie Perkins is beating out her Persian carpet.

CLEMMY: Never get the dust out of that, not in a hundred years.

> *Exit* CLARRY. CECIL *and* EDIE *relay the mat,* CECIL *returns to* EEK, *and they talk shop.* POLLY *sidles up to* JACK *who pretends to ignore her.* EDIE *exits out back.*

JACK: Whadda you hangin' around for, Polly Perkins? I'll give you a chinese burn.

POLLY: Mind your lip, Jack Tuesday. You're as bad as your brother Harry.

JACK: My brother's alright.

POLLY: Your brother's bad.

JACK: Who says so?

POLLY: Everybody knows about bad black Harry, in Fremantle gaol. Everyone that matters.

JACK: Who matters?

> EDIE *re-enters, carrying a bowl of pink roses which she places on the end of the shop counter.*

EDIE: [*calling*] Polly! Polly Perkins, you keep away from the rough end of town or the Flasher'll get you.

> EDIE *joins* EEK *and* CECIL BRUNNER, *backs to the audience, as* CECIL *displays his wares.*

POLLY: [*to JACK*] I saw you kissing Touch of the Tar down the rough end of town.

JACK: That was Harry. She's Harry's girl.

POLLY: It was you, Jack Tuesday. I always know you by the dimple in your cheek.

JACK: [*touched*] Do you, Pol? Anyway, she's gone walkabout with the sandalwood cutters.

> JACK *has been carefully sweeping towards the bowl of roses. He grabs the bunch, puts it behind his back, ditches the broom and whistles back across stage, passing* CLARRY *as she re-enters with her sewing basket.* POLLY *pretends not to notice.*

[*Cheerfully*] Morning, Miss Clarry, Miss Clem.

CLARRY & CLEMMY: Morning, Jack.

JACK: Not a cloud in the sky.

CLARRY & CLEMMY: But so bad for the crops.

> *They all grin conspiratorially.* JACK *brings the roses out in front of his chest.*

JACK: [*awkwardly*] Here, Pol, I picked these for you.

POLLY: [*sweetly*] Oh! You never? Oh! You shouldn't 've. Oh! Jack, they're so pretty.

JACK: Not as pretty as you are.

POLLY: Pretty as Touch of Tar?

JACK: Prettier.

POLLY: [*primly*] Pretty is as pretty does. She puts apples down the front of her dress to make two bulges.

JACK: [*embarrassed*] I know.

POLLY *turns sideways.*

POLLY: If I stand sideways can you see anything?

JACK: See what?

POLLY: A difference?

JACK: Oh!… Since when?

POLLY: Since last time you looked, silly!

JACK *swings her around.*

JACK: Not much.

POLLY *pouts,* JACK *laughs and tries to kiss her clumsily.*

Polly!

POLLY *twists away.*

EDIE: [*calling*] Polly! Put the kettle on!

POLLY: It's time to go in. The midges are biting.

EDIE: And we'll all have tea!

POLLY *dances off.* JACK *comes centre stage for his song, accompanied by* CECIL BRUNNER, EEK *and* EDIE *and the two* MISSES HUMMER. *During the song* POLLY *returns with tea, teacups, milk jug and silver teapot and serves tea.*

'POLLY PUT THE KETTLE ON'

JACK: [*singing*] On Monday mornings in the street
There is a girl I love to meet,
She captures every heart.
The blinds go up, the curtains part,
And nothing could be finer,
And I love her more than all the tea in China.

All sing and dance as POLLY *re-enters.*

ALL: For it's Polly Perkins, pretty Polly Perkins,
All the boys give her the eye.

Pretty Polly Perkins is the girl for me,
So Polly put the kettle on and we'll all have tea.
Hey, Polly!

JACK, CECIL *and* EEK *give long wolf whistles.*

CECIL: In Mukinupin Polly is the Mukinupin belle,
There's not a gal to touch her, I know because I fell
For pretty Polly Perkins when first she caught my eye
And I lingered on the corner just to see her passing by.

ALL: And we lingered on the corner just to see her passing by.

EEK: O she passes by in Mucka with such a lovely air;
Her dress is made of muslin, there's a ribbon in her hair,
And every man in Mucka is leaping to his feet
When little Polly Perkins drops her ribbon in the street.

POLLY *drops her ribbon,* JACK *and* CECIL BRUNNER *scramble for it but* JACK *wins, triumphantly.*

ALL: Hey, Polly!
For it's Polly, Polly Perkins, pretty Polly Perkins.
All the boys in the street are giving her the eye,
Little Polly Perkins is the girl for me,
So Polly put the kettle on and we'll all have tea.
Hey, Polly!

JACK, CECIL *and* EEK *give wolf whistles.* POLLY *passes around the cups. There is laughter, chatting.*

POLLY: Tea, Miss Clarry; tea, Miss Clem. One lump or two?
CLARRY & CLEMMY: Thank you, dearest Polly, don't mind if we do.

Laughter. EDIE PERKINS *comes centre stage to recite, to accompaniment on the piano.*

EDIE: Airy fairy Lilian,
Flitting, fairy Lilian,
When I ask her if she love me
Claps her tiny hands above me,
Laughing all she can;
She'll not tell me if she love me…

ALL: Put her in a billycan.

EDIE: [*oblivious*] Cruel little Lilian…

CECIL BRUNNER *comes forward and bows.*

CECIL: I'm afraid the time has come to say farewell. My good grey mare and sulky are waiting, and I am a knight of the road.

He crosses to POLLY *and kisses her hand.*

Goodbye, Miss Polly, goodbye till next time.

EDIE: Say goodbye to Mr Brunner, Polly.

POLLY: Goodbye, Mr Brunner.

CECIL: Cecil.

He waits but POLLY *only smiles vaguely.*

Dare I hope, Miss Polly? Dare I carry with me on my journey the memory of one dark rose with the dewdrops in her hair?

POLLY *hangs her head,* JACK *clenches his fist.*

EEK: Good stamp of a chap, that Brunner. He'll make a go of it.

CECIL *shakes him by the hand, then pauses before* JACK, *who begins to whistle and look elsewhere.*

Take Mr Brunner's bag, Jack. Hop to it, lad.

CECIL: Goodbye, sweet ladies.

They all wave, JACK *picks up the bag, looking sulky.*

CLARRY & CLEMMY: God speed, Mr Brunner.

CECIL BRUNNER *exits, followed by* JACK. EDIE *stands waving as* CECIL *disappears.* POLLY *puts her tongue out at his retreating back.* EDIE *turns and catches her at it.*

EDIE: Polly Perkins! It's time you put your hair up, my lady, and lengthened your skirts.

EEK *pulls a chair out from behind the counter and sits down to read the paper, his back to the women.* POLLY *props a mirror on the counter and begins to do up her hair, trying different styles.* EDIE *drags out some bolts of material—silks and satins—from behind the counter and staggers downstage with them.*

We'll get Miss Clarry and Miss Clemmy to make you up something stylish. What do you think of this, Miss Clarry?

EDIE *holds a bolt of satin up against* POLLY.

CLARRY: Too old for Polly, Mrs Perkins. Too sophisticated. Don't you think so, Clemmy?

POLLY: But I'd love something sophisticated.

CLEMMY: She needs—stand up, dear—she needs a beaded pink georgette.

POLLY: Ooh, lovely!

POLLY *pulls off her dress, helped by* EDIE, *and stands in her slip.*

CLARRY: Clemmy always had perfect taste, always.

CLEMMY: But you were the dressmaker, dear. I'll always remember how you dressed the divine Sarah.

CLARRY: La dame aux camélias in white, slipper satin.

CLEMMY: You were a goldmine for JCW's. I only hung by my teeth from the Big Top in dyed pink, see-through muslin.

CLARRY: You were a marvel, dear. If only you'd used a net.

CLEMMY: I ascended in a balloon above Melbourne, singing 'tra-la-la-boom-de-ay'.

She begins to sing and attempts a dance.

CLARRY: Fun and music are what the people want, dear.

CLEMMY: After I fell I had a cat, rat and canary show.

CLARRY: In the theatre everything is possible. Stand up here, Polly.

EDIE *brings the pink georgette and a packet of pins.* POLLY *climbs up on the table and slips the pink georgette over her head.* EDIE *stands by with the pins.* CLARRY *kneels at* POLLY'*s hem, pins in her mouth, as* CLEMMY *tries an odd wavery little dance around them, leaning on her crutch. The cries of the two women punctuate* CLEMMY'*s speeches.*

CLARRY & EDIE: [*in turn*] Hold still, Polly! Pull your bottom in! She needs a little pad on her lower spine! But sway-backs are so fashionable! Don't wriggle, Polly! Polly!

POLLY *gives an occasional 'Ouch!' as a pin goes in.*

CLEMMY: Ta-ra-ra-boom-de-ay, ta-ra-ra-boom-de-ay... Remember Annette Kellerman, Clarry, swimming at the Aquarium? And the waxworks in Bourke Street, Baby Bliss the fat lady and the midgets, General and Mrs Mite? You've got a dip in the hem there, dear.

POLLY: Oh! Tell us about it, Miss Clemmy.

CLARRY: Keep still, dear.

CLEMMY: Ta-ra-ra-boom-de-ay, ta-ra-ra-boom-de-ay. Well! We had to cancel Ben Hur because of the bubonic plague but Lillian Russell looked beautiful up to the last till her voice went off, and she had to pay me to sing her finales for her.

POLLY: [*enchanted*] Lillian Russell!

CLEMMY: And Nellie Stewart was principal boy in Cinderella. All the gallery girls called 'Nellie, Nellie!' and threw her floral tributes.

POLLY: [*ecstatic*] Nellie Stewart!

CLEMMY: [*stopping dead*] But then His Majesty's burnt down on a Palm Sunday and I fell from the highwire and ended up... in Mukinupin.

POLLY: Oh! Miss Clemmy, Miss Clemmy, how could you bear it?

CLEMMY: Dead and buried under a sea of scrub.

EDIE: Don't wriggle, Polly.

CLARRY: Almost finished. There! [*She rises stiffly.*] Doesn't she look a picture?

EDIE: Marvellous, Miss Clarry. Marvellous! Such dash, such style, such a waste in Mukinupin.

POLLY: [*getting down*] How do I look, Miss Clemmy?

> CLEMMY *clasps* POLLY *to her.*

CLEMMY: Dearest Polly, you look like... like Gladys Moncrieff in Peg 0' My Heart.

POLLY: Oh! Miss Clemmy, do I, do I?

> POLLY *whirls around the stage.* EDIE *puts up her ear trumpet.*

EDIE: Who? Who?

POLLY: [*whirling EDIE with her*] Gladys Moncrieff, Mummy.

EDIE: She does too, she does too.

> EDIE *rushes across to* EEK *and rattles his paper.*

Father, Father, look at our Polly! She's the spitting image of Gladys Moncrieff.

EEK: Looks like Polly Perkins to me.

> POLLY *dances over to him, hugs and kisses him, laughing.*

POLLY: Dearest Pa, I'm so happy I could... bite your ear off.

> POLLY *dances about singing 'Ta-ra-ra-boom-de-ay'.* EEK *looks pleased, rustles his paper.*

EDIE: Listen to her, hitting a high C like an opera star. Why, even I can hear her.

EEK: The line's gone through to Jiliminning.

EDIE: What's that, Father? Speak up.

EEK: Jiliminning… Line's through!

EDIE: [*proclaiming*] 'The mighty bush with iron rails is tethered to the world'; and our daughter is singing like… Jenny Lind.

EEK: Make a good wife for some steady feller. Says here some Archduke's been assassinated at… some outlandish place.

EDIE: Where?

EEK: Sar-a-jevo.

EDIE: Never heard of it.

CLARRY: Thank God we live in Mukinupin.

CLEMMY: Nothing ever happens here.

POLLY: Summer's ending. I've put my hair up and lengthened my skirts. Everything changes.

> EDIE *exits with the tea things. The sisters sit.* POLLY *comes centre stage for song.*

'SUMMER BIRD'

POLLY: I saw the summer bird
          Blue as the sky,
          That was her song you heard
          Down by the creek she went
          I saw her flying so high,
          Summer bird—fly, summer bird—fly.

          The summer bird is blue,
          Blue as the creek water,
          I'll give her song to you
          If you tell me who taught her
          All the notes in the scale
          And some I've never heard;
          Through winter's frost and hail
          Come back, my summer bird.
          Summer bird—fly, summer bird—fly.

          I'll see the summer bird, blue as the day;

That was her song you heard
Before she flew away into the wattle tree,
Summer bird—fly, summer bird—fly.
Summer bird—fly.

JACK *re-enters triumphantly holding two tickets.*

JACK: Pol, Pol, I've got us two front row tickets for Max and Mercy Montebello for The Strangling of Desdemona in the Mukinupin Town Hall.

POLLY: Oh, Jack! You're a marvel!

POLLY *embraces the delighted* JACK. *General excitement as they all crowd around, except for* EEK *who continues ostentatiously reading his paper, rustling the sheets.*

ALL: The Montebellos!

JACK: In the flesh. And two complimentaries for Miss Clarry and Miss Clemmy Hummer in honour of their long association with the profession.

CLARRY: How thoughtful!

JACK *and* POLLY *rush about setting up the seats outside the Town Hall.*

CLEMMY: They played the Hippodrome in the old days.

CLARRY: I dressed her for Rosalind in those skin-tight, satin breeches. Her figure could take it. She was so lissome. Remember, Clem?

CLEMMY: [*grimly*] The incomparable Mercy. Who could ever forget her!

EEK *stands and reads aloud:*

EEK: August the third, 1914. Should the worst happen after everything has been done that honour will permit, Australians will stand beside our own to defend her to our last man and our last shilling.

No-one takes any notice of him. There is a roll of drums. Enter MAX MONTEBELLO, *very Italian, with a sweeping moustache, wide-brimmed black hat, and a cloak. He stands at the Town Hall entrance and strikes an attitude. There is a breathless hush.*

MAX: Ladies an' gentlemens.

Another drum roll, and a sweeping bow. A pause while EDIE

bundles up EEK, JACK *throws off his apron and takes* POLLY'*s arm, the* MISSES HUMMER *move upstage, arm in arm.*

Actor-Manager Max Montebello presents… fresha from ze triumps in Kununoppin and Koolyanoboff, and under distingué patronage… Madame Mercy Montebello!

Enter MERCY, *a faded beauty in a white nightgown, curtseying grandly.*

Ze world's greatest act-resse in ze Pathétique and Triumphant 'Eroines of Shakespeare, wiz illustrative act-ing of ze varrying emotions of ze great Master's incomparable 'eroines.

The audience clap enthusiastically. MAX *bows.* MERCY *curtseys.* MAX *holds up his hand in a commanding gesture.*

Despite ze vicious rumour, despite ze tragic times, despite Madame's perigrinations aroun' ze bent surface of dis 'oary of planette, I would like to ensure our aud-ience that 'er majestic voice shows absolutely no sign of de wear or de tear.

He gestures at MERCY *and she attempts to hit a high note.*

JACK: You can do better than that, Pol.

MAX *glares but* MERCY *curtseys and smiles winningly again, touching* JACK'*s heart. He leaps to his feet, ashamed.*

[*Gallantly*] Three cheers for Madame Mercy.

Mukinupin claps but POLLY *pulls* JACK *down in his seat, shushing him.* MERCY *exits, blowing kisses to the delighted* JACK.

MAX: Zank you, Zank you, Mukinupin. And now I would like to draw ze attention of ze audience to ze refined presence of Miss Clarice and Miss Clementine; Miss Clarice, once J. C. Williamson's most distingué costumière, Miss Clementine, ze great-est female wire-walker in ze Sousern 'Emisphere.

Much applause as the MISSES HUMMER *rise and bow.*

JACK: [*standing*] Hooray, hooray for Miss Clarry and Miss Clemmy.

MAX: And as ze curtain raiser for ze great tragedy of Mr Shakespeare, our local artiste…

He fumbles for the name. JACK *jumps up and whispers in his ear.*

Ah! Yes… it is… Madame Edee who vill favour us wis one of 'er mosta delightful recitations from ze maudlin bard, ze Poet Laureate, Alfred Lord Tenny-son.

> MAX *bows and withdraws. Excited cries from audience of 'Surprise! Surprise!' as* EDIE, *shoved on stage by* EEK, *rises all smiles and moves centre.*

EDIE: [*very nervously*] 'The May Queen!'

> *Pause for applause but there is none.*

[*Firmly*] 'The May Queen' by Alfred Lord Tennyson.

> *Scattered applause.*

> [*In a rush*] If you're waking call me early, call me early, Mother dear,
> For I would see the sun rise upon the glad New Year,
> It is the last New Year that I shall ever see,
> Then you may lay me low in the mould and think no more of me…

> *Sniffles, loud sobs, and* EEK *blows his nose with vigour.*

> [*Warming to it*] Goodnight, goodnight, when I have said goodnight for evermore,
> And you see me carried out from the threshold of the door;
> Don't let… don't… don't let…

> *She casts about wildly for the word.*

POLLY: [*in a stage whisper*] Effie!
EDIE: Ay?

> *She puts up her ear trumpet.*

POLLY: [*louder*] Effie!
EDIE: Who?
ALL: Effie, Effie, Effie!
EEK: [*bellowing*] For God's sake woman, Effie!
EDIE: [*scornfully*] But I will see the sun rise upon the glad New Year
ALL: So if you're waking, call me, call me early, Mother Dear

> *Applause as* EDIE *returns to her seat and* MERCY *enters in her nightgown, singing.*

MERCY: The poor soul sat sighing by a sycamore tree,
    Sing all a green willow,
    Her hand on her bosom and her head on her knee,
    Sing willow, willow, willow;
    The fresh streams ran by her, and murmur'd her moans,
    Sing willow, willow, willow,
    Her salt tears fell from her, and soften'd the stones;
    Sing willow, willow, willow;
    Sing all a green willow must be my garland,
    Let nobody blame him, his scorn I approve—

Hark, who is't that knocks?
    I call'd my love false love; but what said he then?
    Sing willow, willow, willow;
    If I court moe women, you'll couch with moe men.

Who's there? Othello?
MAX: [*entering, blackface*] Ay, Desdemona.
MERCY: Will you come to bed, my lord?
MAX: 'Ave you pray'd tonight, Desdemona?
MERCY: Ay, my lord.
MAX: If you bethink yourself of any crime
    Unreconcil'd as yet to 'eaven and grace,
    Solicit for it straight.
MERCY: Alas! my lord, what may you mean by that?
MAX: Well, do it, and be brief; I will walk by:
    I woulda not kill zy unprepared spirit,
    No, heaven forfend, I woulda not kill zy soul.
MERCY: Talk you of killing?
MAX: Ay, I do.
MERCY: Then heaven have Mercy on me!
MAX: Amen! Wis all my heart.
MERCY: If you say so, I hope you will not kill me.
MAX: Hum!
MERCY: And yet I fear you; for you are fatal then
    When your eyes roll so.
    Why I should fear I know not,
    Since guiltiness I know not; but yet I feel I fear.
MAX: Zink on zy sins.

MERCY: They are loves I bear to you.

MAX: Ay, and for zat zou diest.

> JACK *hisses loudly, but is restrained by* POLLY.

MERCY: That death's unnatural that kills for loving.
　　Alas! Why gnaw you so your nether-lip?
　　Some bloody passion shakes your very frame;
　　These are portents: but yet, I hope, I hope
　　They do not point on me.

MAX: Peace and be still!

MERCY: I will so: What's the matter?

MAX: Zat hankerchief which I so lov'd and give zee
　　Zou gav'st to Cassio.

MERCY: No, by my life and soul! Send for the man and ask him

MAX: Sweet soul, taka heed, taka heed of perjury;
　　Zou'rt on zy death-bed.

> JACK *leaps to his feet, anguished.*

JACK: No, no!

> POLLY *pulls him down. Everybody shushes him.*

MERCY: Ay, but not yet to die.

MAX: Yes, presently;
　　Zerefore confess zee freely of zy sin;
　　For to deny each article viz oass
　　Cannot remove nor choke ze strong conception
　　Zat I do groan vithal. Zou art to die.

MERCY: Then Lord have mercy on me!

MAX: I say, amen.

MERCY: And have you mercy too! I never did
　　Offend you in my life; never lov'd Cassio
　　But with such general warranty of heaven
　　As I might love; I never gave him token.

MAX: He hath confess'd.

MERCY: What, my Lord?

MAX: That he hath us'd thee.

MERCY: How? Unlawfully?

MAX: Ay.

JACK: It's a lie!

He wrestles with POLLY *to climb over his seat.*

MERCY: He will not say so.

MAX: No; his mouth is stopp'd:

MERCY: What, is he dead? Alas! He is betray'd and I undone.

MAX: Out, strumpet! Weep'st zou for him to my face?

JACK: Villain! Villain!

MERCY: O! Banish me, my lord, but kill me not!

> JACK *weeps loudly.*

MAX: [*put out*] Down, strumpet!

MERCY: [*delighted*] Kill me tomorrow; let me live tonight!

> JACK *thumps the seat.*

JACK: Yes! Yes! Yes!

MAX: [*nervously*] Nay, if you strive—

MERCY: But half an hour!

JACK: [*groaning*] Just half an hour.

MAX: [*glaring*] Being done, zere is no pause.

JACK: Bastard!

MERCY: But while I say one prayer!

MAX: It is too late.

> *He smothers her.* JACK *leaps for the stage.*

JACK: Bloody bastard!

> *He grabs* CLEMMY*'s crutch and charges* MAX *with it. They grapple and roll on the stage.*

MERCY: O! Falsely, falsely murder'd. A guiltless death I die.

JACK: Murder, bloody murder!

> JACK *fetches* MAX *a terrible blow with the crutch.*

MAX: Jesus, Mary and Joseph.

JACK: [*standing over him*] She loved you, cruel Othello.
   Take that and that and this.

> MAX *crawls to* MERCY *and crouches beside her.*

MAX: Oh, bloody period! I kiss'd zee ere I kill'd zee;
   No way but zis,
   Killing myself to die upon a kiss.
   [*In a stage whisper*] O Spartan dog!

MAX *dies, with great fervour.* JACK *stands with crutch upraised. But, unable to control himself, he throws himself over the bodies, weeping. Mukinupin give a standing ovation.*

JACK: O Spartan dog!

MAX *rises, takes* MERCY *by the hand.* MERCY *pulls* JACK *to his feet and rushes him forwards in bow after bow. Gradually* JACK, *realising he is a star too, takes full advantage of the situation, even taking a solo bow. He kisses* MERCY*'s hand, and shakes* MAX*'s hand.*

MAX *quells the audience with a gesture.*

MAX: Zank you. Zank you, Mukinupin. I must say that nevaire before 'ave we 'ad such an extraordinary reception. Zis young man…

MAX *brings* JACK *forward.*

… should 'ave a most remarkable career. I predict great zings for…

He bends to whisper, then holds JACK*'s hand high.*

… for Meestar Jack Toosday.

Applause.

And now, p'raps as a fitting close to zis most wonderful night Mr Toosday may like to entertain you wis zomesing of his own choosing.

He consults JACK.

I give you… Mukinupin's own Mr Zack Toosday in 'An 'Am, an Egg and an Onion'.

JACK *comes forward, abashed, as* MAX *and* MERCY *run offstage hand in hand, and join the audience. But he soon gets back his self-confidence, and begins his song with suitable tap dance accompaniment.*

'AN 'AM, AN EGG AND AN ONION'

JACK: I'd 'ave it for breakfast each mornin'
          If I could I would 'ave it for tea,
          An 'am, an egg and an onion
          Is the fav'rite banquet for me.

I took a job in the city
But when I lined up for me pay,
The boss said 'An egg and an onion
Is all that you're gettin' terday'.

So I said, 'Where's the 'am?'

ALL: So 'e said, 'Where's the 'am?'

JACK: I went out on the town wiv me sweet'eart
The cafe that we went to was naice,
For an 'am and an egg and an onion
But there wasn't an egg in the place.

So I said, 'Where's the egg?'

ALL: So 'e said, 'Where's the egg?'

JACK: I got married last Saturdee arvo',
The missus was cookin' me tea,
There was 'am and an egg but no onion,
She says 'Give up onions for me'.

So I said, 'Where's the onion?'

ALL: So 'e said, 'Where's the onion?'

JACK: I packed all me clobber and 'opped it,
I caught the first train outa town,
For an 'am and an egg and an onion,
I went to a pub and sat down.

No 'am?

ALL: No 'am!

JACK: No egg!

ALL: No egg?!

JACK: No onion!

ALL: No onion?!

JACK: So I went outback on a station,
The cook 'ad been there for years,
Cookin' 'am, cookin' eggs, cookin' onions
Till it all come out of our ears.

'Ave an 'am, 'ave an egg, 'ave an onion,
'E'd say wiv 'is soupy grin,
The bloody crook, it was all 'e could cook,

So i up and clobbered 'im.

Mukinupin, plus the MONTEBELLOS, *dance down the aisle and join* JACK *onstage for the finale.*

ALL: 'Ave an 'am, 'ave an egg, 'ave an onion,
And just for a change if you can,
'Ave an egg, and an 'am and an onion,
Or an onion, an egg and an 'am.

The MISSES HUMMER *dance off,* EEK *and* EDIE *return to the shop,* EEK *behind the counter.* POLLY, JACK, MERCY *and* MAX *are left centre stage on the red carpet.* JACK *leaves* POLLY *alone as* MERCY *beckons him over. She puts her arm round* JACK.

MERCY: Jack Tuesday, if ever you need a job you'll always find one waiting with Max and Mercy Montebello. Isn't that right, Max?

MAX: Thassaright, Mercy.

MERCY: You're a natural, Jack. You're meant for the bright lights. What are you doing in… Mukinupin?

JACK: [*overcome*] I'm a grocer's boy, ma'am, in Perkins' General Store.

MERCY: A grocer's boy! [*Turning to* POLLY] And this is…?

JACK: [*eagerly*] Polly Perkins, ma'am. She's the… storekeeper's daughter.

MERCY: Oh! I… see! And very sweet, very pretty too. H'dy' do, Polly?

    POLLY *curtseys grimly.*

POLLY: Very well, thank you, ma'am.

MERCY: Well, Polly, your Jack's got a great future in the halls. He's wasted here in Mukinupin. Surely even you must see that?

POLLY: [*defensively*] He could work his way up to be manager.

MERCY: Manager! Manager!

    She turns to MAX *and they smile and shrug together.*

Oh, well of course, if that's what he wants. Is that what you want Jack, dear?

JACK: Well… as a matter of fact… [*Looking wildly around*] I couldn't leave Polly.

    MAX *raises his eyes to heaven.*

MAX: He couldn't leava Polly.

JACK: That's right.

MAX & MERCY: He couldn't leava Polly.

MERCY: If you ever change your mind, Jack Tuesday, remember Mercy Monte… is waiting.

> JACK *kisses her outstretched hand and* MAX *and* MERCY *exit.*

POLLY: [*furious*] Mercy Monte is waiting! Why, she's old enough to be your mother.

JACK: [*grinning*] She didn't act like my mother. I think she's sweet on me, Pol.

> JACK *preens himself,* POLLY *is disgusted.*

POLLY: Speaking of mothers, I can see the Widow Tuesday bowling down the main street in a horse and buggy done up with string. It's your ma, Jack.

JACK: [*groaning*] Oh, Gawd!

POLLY: And I bet both my button-up boots she's come about the mortgage once again.

> JACK *takes up his broom, puts on his apron and begins sweeping vigorously. Enter* THE WIDOW TUESDAY *dressed in widow's weeds, with a heavy black veil. She sweeps up to* EEK *behind his counter and falls on her knees, in a Dickensian travesty.*

WIDOW TUESDAY: Foreclose, Ezekial Perkins! Fore-close, and put me out of my misery.

EDIE: [*harshly*] Get up, Mrs Tuesday.

EEK: [*testily*] Please get up, Mrs Tuesday.

WIDOW TUESDAY: I am the Widow Tuesday, Mrs Tuesday no longer. Mr Tuesday 'as gone to 'is reward.

> EDIE *puts up her ear trumpet.*

EDIE: What's that, Mrs Tuesday?

WIDOW TUESDAY: [*screaming*] Mr Tuesday is no more.

EDIE: [*grimly*] Drank himself to death, I'll be bound. Well, we can't be held responsible.

WIDOW TUESDAY: I throw myself on your mercy, Eek Perkins. I grovel at the usurer's feet.

JACK: Aw, give it a rest, Ma.

EEK: I'm not a hard man.

WIDOW TUESDAY: 'Earts 'ard as flint and stonier.

EDIE: [*complacently*] We all suffer.

EEK: What about your sons… Widow Tuesday?

WIDOW TUESDAY: Young 'Arry and young Jack? Should the sins of the fathers be visited upon the children, Eek Perkins?

POLLY: Of course not, Pa.

EDIE: Hold your tongue, Miss.

WIDOW TUESDAY: [*moving to chair*] My 'Arry's detained.

EEK: At His Majesty's pleasure?

EDIE: Who?

EEK: [*shouting*] Harry Tuesday… got two years.

WIDOW TUESDAY: 'Arry is as 'Arry does, but my Jack's 'is mother's boy.

JACK: Aw, Ma, put a sock in it.

EEK: Jack's not a bad boy, but he doesn't keep his place. He has… aspirations.

WIDOW TUESDAY: Towards whom?

EEK: Towards our daughter; towards Polly, Widow Tuesday.

WIDOW TUESDAY: [*with heavy sarcasm*] I'd never 'ave believed it. Is it true, Jack?

JACK: Is what true, Ma?

WIDOW TUESDAY: That you and Polly Perkins…?

JACK: Are in love? Why, yes it is true. [*Grinning*] There, it's the first time I've come right out and said it.

EEK: It can't be allowed.

EDIE: Said what?

JACK: [*singing*] I'm in love with Polly Perkins,
    I'm in love with Polly Perkins.

> JACK *waltzes with the broom, then throws it away, and takes* POLLY *in his arms. They waltz together.*

I'm in love with Polly Perkins and she's in love with me,
Pretty Polly Perkins is my fatality,
She's like a rose in summer, her pink cheeks all abloom,
Lovely Polly Perkins illuminates the room.

> JACK *falls on one knee as* POLLY *circles him.*

I cannot live without her, she makes the landscape glow,
Pretty Polly Perkins…

EEK, WIDOW TUESDAY & EDIE: No. No. No.

JACK: No?

POLLY: No?

EEK: Never, Jack Tuesday.

EDIE: She's just put her hair up.

WIDOW TUESDAY: She's too young, Jack.

> JACK *turns to* POLLY.

JACK: Polly?

POLLY: Not yet, Jack. I'm too young. I've… just put my hair up. [*Moving towards him*] Oh, Jack.

> JACK *takes her face in his hands.*

JACK: Lovely Pol, if you don't marry me I'll enlist in the W.A. Light Horse and go to Palestine.

> POLLY *clasps her hands.*

POLLY: And be a hero. Oh, Jack!

EDIE: [*reciting*] Then up spake brave Horatius,
> The captain of the gate,
> To every man upon this earth
> Death cometh soon or late,
> And how can man die better
> Than facing fearful odds,
> For the ashes of his fathers,
> And the temple of his gods?

WIDOW TUESDAY: Don't you go puttin' the mocker on my Jack.

> *She takes out a large white handkerchief and weeps copiously.* EEK *pats her shoulder.*

EEK: There, there…

EDIE: Tears, idle tears.

WIDOW TUESDAY: Idle, are they? Well, let me tell you, Mrs Perkins, or whatever you calls y'self, if you'd a had my sorrows you'd never stop bawlin'. I was a civilised 'uman bein' before Mr Tuesday brought me to this God forsakin' 'ole.

EEK: Character and success go hand in hand.

WIDOW TUESDAY: [*darkly*] Mr Tuesday was never much of a mixer and there's some I would never 'ave mixed with, in the old days.

EDIE: What's that?

EEK: [*shouting*] There's some she'd never have mixed with!

EDIE: Who?

WIDOW TUESDAY: There's some as is no better than they should be.

EEK: [*brightly*] Price of wheat going up, price of wool firming.

WIDOW TUESDAY: Some 'as got skeletons in their cupboards... and they're not white ones.

EEK: [*desperately*] Go home and you'll find there's been a thunderstorm.

WIDOW TUESDAY: [*gloomily*] Rust and moth, moth and rust. Mr Tuesday was a good provider, swallered a packet of Aspros every mornin', and shot 'isself through the 'ead goin' rabbitin'. There was no blot on 'is escutcheon.

EDIE: No what?

EEK: [*bellowing*] No blood, I mean, no blot on his escutcheon!

EDIE: Who's escutcheon?

WIDOW TUESDAY: If the cap fits, wear it. I've 'ad me say.

EEK: [*desperately*] I'll take out a second mortgage, Widow Tuesday. Always ready to help a battler.

WIDOW TUESDAY: You've got your head screwed on right, Mr Perkins, and God will reward yous.

EDIE: What she say?

EEK: God will reward us!

WIDOW TUESDAY: God 'elps them as 'elps themselves. Comin', Jack?

> JACK *moves across from* POLLY *to take his mother's arm.*

POLLY: Spring's coming. I can hear the buggy wheels turning into the street for the tennis court dance.

JACK: Save the last one for me... the lights-out dance.

> POLLY *smiles.* JACK *exits with* WIDOW TUESDAY. POLLY *tries a few dance steps.*

POLLY: [*singing*] I'm in love with Jackie Tuesday
> And he's in love with me.
> Handsome Jackie Tuesday
> Is my fatality.

> I cannot live without him,
> He makes the landscape glow,

I don't want to lose him,
And I don't want him to go.

Enter CECIL BRUNNER *with sample case.*

EDIE: Why, it's Mr Brunner. You remember Mr Brunner, Polly?

POLLY: Of course, Mother.

CECIL: Why, Miss Polly, you're quite the gracious lady. How time does fly.

POLLY: Thank you, Mr Brunner.

CECIL: Why don't you call me Cecil?

EDIE: Yes, why don't you call him Cecil?

CECIL: Please don't stand on ceremony.

POLLY: I don't want to be too familiar.

CECIL: But I want you to be too familiar.

POLLY: I'm a nice girl, Mr Brunner.

CECIL: Cecil.

POLLY: Cecil.

CECIL: Dare I hope—Polly?

POLLY: Hope for what?

CECIL: That you'll have another acid drop.

POLLY: Don't mind if I do.

While CECIL *and* POLLY *begin their song,* EDIE *is going through his samples, holding up petticoats and nightgowns.*

'HAVE ANOTHER ACID DROP'

CECIL: Have another acid drop—
POLLY: Don't mind if I do.
CECIL: Take another acid drop,
          Promise to be true.

          I'm a knight upon the road,
          Flogging lingerie,
          I sell the stuff of romance
          In a corset and toupée.

POLLY *and* EDIE *are exclaiming over a trousseau-type negligée.*
POLLY *pulls her dress off and with* EDIE'*s help tries it on.*

          As I move about the country,
          The salt lakes and the scrub,

> There's a mirage that haunts me
> In every outback pub.
>
> When I fold up my corset,
> And take off my toupée,
> There's little Polly Perkins
> In my lingerie.

POLLY: I'm little Polly Perkins
           In a white negligée.

CECIL: I give a rosebud to her,
           And beg her to be true,
           I offer her an acid drop

POLLY: Don't mind if I do.

CECIL: But when I wake at daybreak,
           I know the bird has flown,
           Little Polly Perkins
           Will never be my own.

> So take a case of samples,
> Take a rose bouquet,
> Take a heart and wear it
> On your white negligée.
>
> Take another acid drop,
> Tell me you'll be true,
> Have another acid drop.

POLLY: Don't mind if I do.

POLLY whirls about the room in her new negligée while CECIL *talks to* EDIE, *showing off his wares upstage.* JACK *has re-entered during the song and stands downstage left, glowering at* POLLY.

JACK: Take it off.
POLLY: Why?
JACK: It's… indecent, that's why.
POLLY: Why?
JACK: Because it… shows.
POLLY: Shows what?
JACK: Everything!
POLLY: Don't you like it?
JACK: No.

POLLY: Liar!

JACK: He gave it to you.

POLLY: Mr Brunner.

JACK: [*mocking*] Cecil!

POLLY: He likes me.

JACK: D'ya want to be an old man's darlin'?

POLLY: I'm not an old man's—anything.

JACK: Then take it off.

POLLY: No. I'm not a young man's—anything, either.

JACK: I thought you was.

POLLY: Then you thought wrong. Mother says—

JACK: [*mocking*] Mother says!

POLLY: You're too… familiar.

JACK: You didn't used to think so.

POLLY: When?

JACK: Behind the flour sacks in the storeroom after closin' time.

POLLY: You're not a gentleman.

JACK: Mother says!

POLLY: I shouldn't waste myself.

JACK: [*angry*] Don't, then.

POLLY: I don't intend to.

>   *She tosses her head.*

JACK: You'll soon be rid of me.

POLLY: What's that mean?

JACK: Miss Polly with her hair up.

POLLY: [*hurt*] Don't you like it, either?

JACK: It's nothin' to me.

POLLY: That's alright, then.

>   *She turns away.*

JACK: I got other fish, bigger fish…

POLLY: What, then?

JACK: Joined up.

POLLY: Joined up!

>   *She turns back.*

JACK: Goin' to the war… [*a laugh*] to be a hero.

POLLY: What for?

JACK: To fight the Hun. Better than a grocer's boy. Or a—nightie traveller.

POLLY: You're not going.

She crosses and confronts him.

JACK: Goodbye, Polly.

He takes off his apron and begins to move away.

POLLY: Come back.

JACK: Can't come back. The war'll be over in a month or two.

CECIL: England needs you, Jack.

EEK: The only good German is a dead German.

EDIE: Keep clean and fight fairly.

Re-enter the two MISSES HUMMER *with a large Australian flag. They stand downstage well in view and wave it. As* JACK *puts on his army uniform, slouch hat and leather leggings and hoists his kitbag on his shoulder,* EEK, EDIE, CECIL *and* POLLY *dance and sing him off to the war. The two* MISSES HUMMER *join in the singing.*

'YOUR COUNTRY NEEDS YOU IN THE TRENCHES'

ALL: [*except JACK*] Your country needs you in the trenches,
    Follow your masters into war,
    And if you cop it we'll remember you
    At the Mukinupin Store.

    Economic domination
    That's what we're fighting for,
    Join up and save the Empire,
    We've got to win the war.

    You'll murder them at Wipers.
    And at Bathsheba Wells,
    Only one more stunt, boys,
    And then you'll get a spell.

    Face the test of nationhood,
    Keep Australia free,
    England needs you, Jack, to fight
    For me, and me, and me.

> Your country needs you in the trenches,
> Follow your masters into war,
> And if you cop it we'll remember you
> At the Mukinupin store.

> And if you cop it we'll remember you
> At the Mukinupin store.

EDIE & POLLY: Your mothers and your sisters,
> Your sweethearts and your wives,
> Won't hand you a white feather,
> If you'll only look alive.

EEK & CECIL: Look alive, for Chrissake look alive,
> The brasshats are all toffs,
> But we've gotta beat the Boch,
ALL: For England Home and Beauty look alive.
> Your country needs you in the trenches,
> Follow your masters into war
> And if you cop it we'll remember
> You at the Mukinupin Store.

EEK: Fight for the West, laddie.

JACK: The West, why it's the freest, richest, happiest land on earth. I'll fight for it.

As JACK *exits waving,* POLLY *sobs,* EDIE *with her arm around* POLLY *recites:*

EDIE: Hail beauteous land, hail bonzer Western Australia,
> Compared to ye all others are a failure.

They all cheer. POLLY *tears herself away and runs after* JACK.

POLLY: Come back, Jack... Oh! Please... come back.

Her voice breaks and she exits, running. EEK *and* CECIL *exit through the shop, but* EDIE *lingers, looking after* POLLY, *shading her eyes against the setting sun.*

EDIE: [*reciting*] The red sun sinks in the springtime heat
> And waves of shadow go over the wheat.

A pause, then EDIE *calls, as if to a child:*

Polly, Polly Perkins, keep away from the rough end of town, speak when you're spoken to, and then only to the Bank Manager's daughter.

She exits through the shop and the MISSES HUMMER *are left, staring dreamily into the evening,* CLARRY *with the Australian flag draped across her knees. Very faintly the weird night music begins on the soundtrack.* CLEMMY *stands leaning on her stick looking into the distance.*

CLARRY: [*softly*] Red sky at morning, shepherd's warning.

CLEMMY: [*whispering*] Red sky at night, shepherd's delight. [*Pause.*] I think I can smell rain.

CLARRY: You're always imagining things, Clem.

The night sounds begin as the stage darkens... A last crow calls, a dingo howls, an insect begins tapping; there is a wolf whistle, a coo-ee, then a wild scream. CLARRY *starts up.*

What's that?

CLEMMY: Don't be a fool, Clarry. It's only the Flasher down in the creek bed.

CLARRY: [*relieved*] And the girls giggling under the pepper trees, holding hands.

CLEMMY: [*darkly*] The blacks like wild ducks crying under the guns.

There is a change of tone now which CLARRY *has been fighting off.*

CLARRY: [*faintly*] The sky was full of crows... wasn't it?

CLEMMY: And arsenic in the waterholes.

There is a quavering voice a long way off.

ZEEK: [*off*] Water... Water... Water...

CLARRY: [*alarmed again*] Who's that?

CLEMMY: You know who it is.

CLARRY: [*relieved*] Zeek Perkins... of course, it's only old Zeek.

CLEMMY: It's the dowser... looking for stars and water.

CLARRY: [*sympathetically*] He hasn't been right since he did that perish in the desert, and they brought him in with the skin shrivelled off him like bacon rind. They said he followed a mirage for days, crawling naked under the sun. That was an awful thing, Clem.

Enter ZEEK *dressed in ragged clothes, barefoot, with a cabbage-tree hat and a long white beard. He carries a hurricane lantern, a waterbag and a diviner's rod. On his back is strapped a primitive telescope. He looks a mysterious, yet benign, figure.*

ZEEK: Water, water, everywhere, but not a drop to drink.

CLARRY: Goodnight, Zeek Perkins.

ZEEK *moves in a circle around the stage pointing his diviner's rod at the earth.*

ZEEK: Bad water... too much salt in it.

CLARRY: [*standing*] It's late and I'm going to bed, and so would you, Clem, if you had the sense you were born with.

CLEMMY: I'm not sleepy.

CLARRY: [*moving off*] No more of it.

CLEMMY: [*innocently*] No more of what?

CLARRY: Take care, Clemmy, please take care.

CLEMMY *smiles mysteriously.* POLLY*'s voice is heard in the distance.*

POLLY: [*offstage, calling*] Jack... Jack... Come back, Jack...

CLARRY *exits. The mysterious night music begins again. There is a loud wolf whistle and* POLLY *runs on, calling...*

Jack! Jack!

ZEEK *is setting up his telescope.* POLLY *runs to him.*

Oh! Uncle Zeek, you haven't seen Jack Tuesday tonight, have you?

ZEEK: The river of the water of life is bright as crystal. If anyone thirst, let her come to me.

POLLY: I have come to you.

She shakes his arm.

Uncle Zeek, where's Jack Tuesday?

ZEEK *guides her to the telescope.*

ZEEK: [*confiding*] Look in there, Polly, there's deserts and stars and the five days of creation.

POLLY: [*half-crying*] I don't want your deserts and stars. I want Jack.

ZEEK *grips her arm so fiercely that she cries out.*

ZEEK: Then drink, Polly... drink fire, blood, sand and water.

ZEEK forces her head back and tips the waterbag towards her mouth. POLLY chokes on the water, and struggles away.

POLLY: You're just a crazy old man.

ZEEK: [*still pouring the water out*] You can run it through an hour glass.

POLLY: An old humbug, who knows nothing, Nothing, do you hear?

But ZEEK has lost interest in her. He has his eye to the telescope. POLLY turns away, raging, and sees CLEMMY watching her. She runs to CLEMMY.

Oh, Miss Clemmy, how glad I am to see you! I'm looking for Jack Tuesday, and I can't get any sense out of anybody.

CLEMMY: [*silkily*] Why, dearest Polly, what's the matter?

POLLY: [*in tears*] My Jack's gone, Miss Clemmy. He's gone to the war without saying goodbye or anything.

CLEMMY: [*innocently*] But why?

POLLY: Because he thinks I don't love him anymore. But he's wrong. He's terribly wrong. Of course I love him.

CLEMMY: Do you, Polly?

POLLY: Yes, yes I do. I'm sure I do.

CLEMMY: You're too young to know anything about love.

POLLY: Of course I'm not. How can you say that? I'm exactly the right age to fall in love. I just want him... to wait a little.

CLEMMY grabs POLLY's arm cruelly.

CLEMMY: Silly Polly Perkins. What's love? Is this... love?

CLEMMY knocks hard on the stage with her crutch. The night sounds and the weird music augment each other. THE FLASHER leaps onstage in a long, ragged overcoat, felt hat pulled down low over his eyes. POLLY is pushed towards him by CLEMMY.

The Mukinupin Flasher!

FLASHER: [*whispering*] Look Polly! Look Polly! Look Polly!

He gives a great leap, opens his coat wide and shuts it again, giggling. POLLY screams.

Look, Polly. Did you ever see such a whopper?

He flashes again.

POLLY: [*crying*] Uncle Zeek, Uncle Zeek, can't you see what's happening?

ZEEK: [*to telescope*] There is a chaos of waters, but the waters of chaos are the waters of life.

> THE FLASHER *circles* POLLY.

FLASHER: [*chanting*] My mother said I never should
  Play with the Flasher in the wood.
  If I did, she would say
  Naughty girl to disobey.
Look Polly! Look Polly! Look!

> POLLY *sinks to her knees, moaning.*

POLLY: Miss Clemmy, Miss Clemmy!

> CLEMMY *puts her hand heavily on* POLLY'*s shoulder.*

CLEMMY: Polly Perkins, you've strayed down the wrong end of town after dark, so now you're going to get more than you bargained for.

> *The* FLASHER *droops in the corner, like a crow, waiting.* ZEEK *stands stiffly, mesmerised beside his telescope.* CLEMMY *knocks imperiously with her crutch.*

> THE WIDOW TUESDAY *enters, gaunt and heavily veiled, like Death.*

WIDOW TUESDAY: [*chanting*] Moth and rust... Rust and moth...

POLLY: Oh! Widow Tuesday, please save me, please.

WIDOW TUESDAY: Don't ask me to pity you, Polly Perkins.

POLLY: For Jack's sake.

WIDOW TUESDAY: Mr Tuesday was dragged ten miles in the stirrup with a bullet through 'is skull. [*She gives an awful scream of demoniac laughter, and a great leap in the air.*] And we all got the barcoo rot.

> *She doubles up with more laughter but* CLEMMY *knocks again for silence and the bullroarers, the didgeridoos and the tapping sticks begin. They rise in intensity as the music grows louder and* THE WIDOW TUESDAY, *with a wild scream, begins to chase* THE FLASHER *(flashing as he runs),* ZEEK *and* POLLY *round and round in a mad game of tag. The music stops abruptly,* THE FLASHER *is left standing centre stage. He takes a matchbox out of his pocket, shakes it and puts it to his ear.*

FLASHER: Down in the creek bed I have found the secret of perpetual motion. I fasten the earphones to my head. I listen to the wireless waves. Marconi the Great one, speak to me! [*He rattles the matchbox and whispers:*] Marconi, Marconi, must I kill?

> *He pauses with a sly look, then with a wild yell he throws off his raincoat and in a flapping white nightshirt chases* POLLY, *the* WIDOW *and* ZEEK *round and round in a counter circle.*

Marconi, Marconi, must I kill?

> THE FLASHER *stops abruptly, puts the matchbox to his ear and shakes it.*

Marconi, Marconi… [*He begins to whimper, then loudly:*] Marconi, Marconi [*a whisper*] must I kill?

> *They all stand poised for flight.*

[*Smiling*] Marconi says I must not frighten the ladies. Marconi says…

> *The music changes, becoming more sinister, the bullroarer insistent.*

ALL: [*chanting in a circle*] We have come over the mire and moss,
　　　　To dance a round with the hobby hoss,
　　　　Sing heigh down down with a derry down-ay,
　　　　Come in, come in, thou hobby hoss.
CLEMMY: Bring in the hobby!
WIDOW TUESDAY: [*screaming*] Bring in old ball!

> *She slaps her thighs, jigging on the spot. With a leap and a skirl of sound the* HOBBY HORSE *enters. The* HOBBY *(*HARRY TUESDAY*) wears a simulated horse's skull on a broomstick, with glass bottles for eye sockets, and a lolling red tongue. He wears a long cloak, so that he appears to be prancing or galloping, and is about eight feet high.*

ALL: [*screaming*] The hobby! The hobby!

> *The* HOBBY *pretends to bite the women, nudging up their skirts, paying particular attention to* POLLY. *All except* CLEMMY *flee from the* HOBBY. *He pursues the terrified* POLLY, *who, half-fainting, is swept into his arms. As they chant the 'Hobby Song' the* HOBBY *exits running, carrying* POLLY, *pursued by* THE FLASHER.

FLASHER: Marconi, Marconi, must I kill?

They exit. ZEEK *moves back to his telescope, chanting.*

ZEEK: Fire and brimstone, fables and fancies.

With a roll of drums, CLEMMY *comes centre stage.* THE WIDOW
TUESDAY *throws down a coil of rope.*

WIDOW TUESDAY: Clemmy Hummer, the greatest female highwire
walker in the world!

THE WIDOW TUESDAY *claps madly. To the drums rising in a
crescendo* CLEMMY *walks gingerly across the wire, wavers,
but goes on. A foot slips, she falls with a terrible scream and
crumples on the stage. The* WIDOW *runs forward, helps her up,
returns her crutch and assists her to the wicker chair.*

CLEMMY: I used to balance on a rope amongst the stars.

ZEEK: Sun, moon and stars, all sweet things.

HARRY TUESDAY *re-enters as himself, dressed in tight-fitting
moleskin trousers and a black Jackie Howe singlet. He has a
rifle and ammunition slung across his body, carries a bottle of
beer in one hand, and the Hobby's head in the other. He is* JACK
TUESDAY*'s identical twin in looks but there the resemblance
ends.* HARRY *is wild, drunken, and full of bitterness.*

HARRY: Grog shops closed, no more fun and games.

HARRY *sits on the edge of the stage.*

CLEMMY: You didn't frighten her too much, did you Harry?

HARRY: No… just give 'er a bit of a thrill, that's all. She'll think she
had a nightmare.

WIDOW TUESDAY: When did you get back, son?

HARRY: Stole a horse and rode inter town ternight.

WIDOW TUESDAY: Dad's dead. Shot himself through the head.

HARRY: The old timers always reckoned anybody was mad took up
land east of the rabbit-proof.

CLEMMY: Tell us about Fremantle, Harry. Tell us a story.

'HARRY TUESDAY'S SONG'

HARRY: The bloody stones they break your bones,
               Inside Fremantle yard;

And it's a curse, there's nothin' worse
Than doin' two years hard.

I killed a sheep, 'twoud make you weep,
For need of a coupla pence,
I kept the law and hung the fleece
Out on the squatter's fence.

The squatter is a stingy man
For stealin' of his ewes,
Inside the yard you'll do it hard,
Kowtowin' to the screws.

The judge will throw you in the can,
He will not grant no bail,
And you can rot till you're forgot
Inside Fremantle gaol.

When I came out then I had nought,
Not a pocketful of pence,
So now I kill and eat me fill,
Hang nothin' on the fence.

Me boots are full of mud and blood,
Me coat is stiff with pain,
I'll never shear the bloody sheep
Out on the One Tree Plain.

But one dark night I'll start a fight,
I'll wake the silent town,
I'll give the law a little fright,
I'll shoot the bastards down.

I won't forget and they'll regret
They give me two years' hard,
To break me bones acrackin' stones
Inside Fremantle yard.

THE WIDOW TUESDAY *beats her thigh with enthusiasm.*

WIDOW TUESDAY: Good on you, son, you're not a crawler like young Jack.
HARRY: Where's Touch of the Tar?
WIDOW TUESDAY: Reckon she went bush.

HARRY: You seen 'er, Miss Clemmy?

CLEMMY: No, Harry. After you were gaoled she left home.

HARRY: Pissed off with a bloody sandalwood cutter, I bet. She always 'ad a weakness for sandalwood. Liked the blue flames. Her and me usta sit and... make up pictures... in the fire... y'know?

ZEEK: Avoid the tail of the Scorpion, but the Wolf will burn forever.

HARRY: [*half-laughing*] That old bastard hits the nail on the head too often. Gooday, matey, what you see in there?

ZEEK: The Cross is a timepiece, Harry, a guide to travelling men. By May it is upright, by August it slopes to the sou'-west, as the earth rolls. Come, take a look in here, my son, and you will see.

HARRY *crosses and takes the telescope.*

HARRY: [*squinting up*] Think I could foller Touch of the Tar with this thing?

ZEEK: The Clouds of Magellan are often lost in the dreaming.

HARRY *hands the telescope back to him with a laugh.*

HARRY: It's a big world up there, old timer. And a hard one down here.

WIDOW TUESDAY: Come on home, Harry. It'll be just like old times, you and me, with the boiled wheat and the roo in the camp oven.

HARRY: Jesus, Ma! What a homecomin'.

WIDOW TUESDAY: You don't need that girl. She's black.

HARRY: Half black. Comes from good white stock. [*Laughing*] They reckon she was fathered by Eek Perkins. She's a boong-basher's daughter.

WIDOW TUESDAY: I got another mortgage out of the ol' bugger by hintin' I knew more than I ought to.

HARRY: Ah, everybody knows, but nobody's sayin'. Bush towns are like that.

ZEEK: [*to his telescope*] The crows are fatted with the murrion flock.

HARRY: Yeah. They reckon of Eek spent a lotta time down in the creek bed with them gins, before he took up murderin' 'em, an' become a lay preacher. [*He doubles up with mirth.*] Y'know, me and him 've got a lot in common. Oh, I know what they call me—a kombo and a gin jockey—but I don't give a stuff. I never went after 'em with guns—not yet, anyway—and Touch of the Tar, she's just right for a gaolbird.

CLEMMY: She's a good girl, Harry.

HARRY: Maybe...

CLEMMY: And she likes you.

HARRY: She don't like me, she loves me, and that means she hates me more than half the time. Well... maybe she's gone for good, and I won't weep over 'er. [*He moves restlessly away as if listening for someone.*] But where is the black bitch? [*Pause.*] How's ol' Jack? Still counter jumpin'?

WIDOW TUESDAY: Gone for a soldier. Left me on me own with the farm and a second mortgage.

HARRY: Did he now? Never thought he had the guts. But a King and Country man, a' course. Well, that's Jack all over. He always fell for the bullshit.

WIDOW TUESDAY: Come home, Harry love, now that you've seen the world...

HARRY: From Fremantle gaol.

WIDOW TUESDAY: You can take up the shearin' again. You're the only gun shearer east of the rabbit-proof.

HARRY: Come 'ome, back ter Stinkwort Holler, not me, Ma. Jack's a joined up. I'll do the same. He's got the right idea for once. Get away from the tattletales, see the world, put a bullet in a few bastards.

The WIDOW *begins to weep noisily.*

So long, Miss Clemmy.

He kisses her awkwardly.

You won't see Harry Tuesday till he comes home a hero.

He grins and takes the WIDOW*'s arm.*

Goodbye, Zeek.

ZEEK: We'll miss you, Harry lad.

HARRY: Say goodbye to Touch of the Tar for me. Tell 'er to be true. [*He doubles up at his own joke.*] C'mon, Ma. Dry your crocodile tears, and help me pack me clobber.

Exit HARRY *and the weeping* WIDOW TUESDAY.

ZEEK: [*into the telescope*] Hercules is well down towards the north with Lyra the harp and Cygnus the swan.

Enter TOUCH OF THE TAR, *a dark beauty in a ragged dress, torn across one breast, with bare, dirty feet.*

TOUCH OF THE TAR: You seen 'Arry Toosday ternight, Miss Clemmy?

CLEMMY: He's just left with his ma.

TOUCH OF THE TAR: [*bitterly*] Two years and don't give a damn about me.

CLEMMY: He asked after you.

TOUCH OF THE TAR: Arsed after me did 'e, the bastard? 'E knows where ter find me. Our ol' place… in the creek bed.

CLEMMY: He's gone for a soldier.

TOUCH OF THE TAR *whistles.*

TOUCH OF THE TAR: Sweet J-e-s-us! What come over 'Arry? 'E only fights when 'e's shickered. [*Mournfully*] Never even said goodbye or up your bum.

CLEMMY: He left a message.

TOUCH OF THE TAR: [*eagerly*] What?

CLEMMY: 'Say goodbye to Touch of the Tar for me.' He thought you'd followed the sandalwood cutters.

TOUCH OF THE TAR: [*bitterly*] Did 'e? Thought I'd gone orf like any ol' black woman. Don' 'e know who I am. I'm Lily Perkins. They reckons me daddy slept with every coloured woman in the camp. [*Pause.*] Trouble with me is, Miss Clemmy, it's give me ideas. I 'xpect too much for a coloured girl, don' I?

During this dialogue JACK *has entered and slumps on the Town Hall steps. He is very drunk. He hiccups.*

[*Sharply*] Wassat?

CLEMMY: [*softly*] Somebody just came in.

TOUCH OF THE TAR: [*delighted*] 'Arry. [*She runs across, stops, hesitates. Shyly.*] That you, 'Arry?

No answer. She moves closer, shaking his arm.

'Arry!

JACK: It's not Harry, it's Jack.

TOUCH OF THE TAR: [*disappointed*] I thought you was 'Arry.

JACK: People sometimes do, but not for long. [*Pause.*] Sorry!

TOUCH OF THE TAR: You look lonely.

JACK: I am… and drunk.

TOUCH OF THE TAR: You like me leedle bit, Jack?

JACK: [*uncomfortably*] Dunno… maybe.

TOUCH OF THE TAR: You like ter come wiv me… down the creek bed somewhere? 'Ave a go?

JACK: Why?

TOUCH OF THE TAR: [*bitterly*] 'Cause they reckon I'm hot bitch: y'know, take on anythin'.

JACK: Don't sell y'self short.

TOUCH OF THE TAR: Why not? I'm nothin'!

JACK: [*gently*] Touch of the Tar…

TOUCH OF THE TAR: Don't call me that. I'm Lily… tha's me name… Lily. Pretty, ain't it?

JACK: [*humbly*] I didn't know.

TOUCH OF THE TAR: No, nobody does, much, an' if they ever did they forgotten. Mind you, it's not me ol' people's name. Tha's another one altogether.

JACK: Old people?

TOUCH OF THE TAR: Ol' people, me mumma's people, but they all gone. Nothin' left now, few gnamma 'oles, stone tools, scarred trees, ol' junk thas all, nothin'. Sometimes I 'ear 'em on the wind.

JACK: [*uneasy*] Hear what?

TOUCH OF THE TAR: 'Ear 'em, cryin' an' screamin', y'know. They reckon they was done in, down the creek bed, fulla bones. Me bastard daddy was in on that. Ever seen 'em?

JACK: No.

TOUCH OF THE TAR: Come wiv me. I'll show you.

JACK: I don't wanta. [*Pause.*] I'm waitin' for a lift.

TOUCH OF THE TAR: Scared, are you?

JACK: No. I'm goin' to the war. I got pissed, that's all.

TOUCH OF THE TAR: Then… come.

> *Slowly, as if mesmerised,* JACK *is pulled across the stage by* TOUCH OF THE TAR.

You'll like it, Jackie, you see. You call me, go on, you say 'Lily'.

JACK: Lily.

TOUCH OF THE TAR: You drunk now, but later… you won't mind. You say it agen… 'Lily'.

JACK: Lily.

TOUCH OF THE TAR: See. Nice, ain't it? Come on, Jack, I'll take care of you. It's nice... in the creek bed. Warm an' dark an' soft, she-oak trees: real nice for us. You'll see.

They exit.

ZEEK: Observe the transit of Venus across the face of the sun.

CLEMMY *sits dozing in her wicker chair. A voice is heard off, approaching and reciting mournfully.*

EDIE: Where fled the quarry, leaping
By hill and creek and plain,
They lie together, sleeping,
The hunter and the slain.

Enter EDIE *in long white calico nightgown, sleep-walking and wringing her hands. She circles the stage.* CLEMMY *wakes, startled.*

Wash your hands, put on your nightgown, don't look so pale.

ZEEK: Where hast thou been, sister. Killing swine?

EDIE: Never again from the night, the night that has taken,
Shall ever the tribes return to tell us their tale,
They lie in a sleep, whence none shall ever awaken...

She washes her hands as she walks.

Here's the smell of the blood still.

ZEEK: And all will vanish, stars, gas, dust, planets, moons.

EDIE: Driven to drown in the swamps—but the wind their dirge; the hunted of the dogs: [*in her ordinary voice*] and now you're a black dog and I'm damned, damned.

ZEEK: The large dog Sirius and the little dog, Canis Minor, mark how they move.

CLEMMY: [*firmly*] Go to bed now, Edie Perkins.

EDIE: To bed, to bed; come, come, come, come, give me your hand, Eek Perkins. What's done can't be undone. Their blood is black on our hands, that nothing can purge.

EDIE *exits, still asleep. Enter* CLARRY *in dressing-gown and hair curlers with night light in her hand.*

CLARRY: [*fearfully*] Are you there, Clemmy? What was that?

CLEMMY: Only Edie Perkins sleepwalking again. I told her to go to bed.

CLARRY: I thought she'd got over it.

CLEMMY: Not as bad as she used to be. It was on every couple of weeks once.

CLARRY: Poor thing! [*Sitting*] To carry that guilty conscience all the days of your life.

CLEMMY: She drove him to it.

CLARRY: Out of wicked jealousy. 'Get rid of the black heathens', she screamed at him, and he did.

CLEMMY: All of them were in it, the whole town, egged on by the wives. And now there's only Touch of the Tar—I mean Lily Perkins—to remind *them*.

CLARRY: It got out of hand.

ZEEK: [*babbling*] The creek ran with blood. 'Come on,' Eek shouted, 'grab your gun', but I took my telescope and went the other way. Some of 'em run out over the salt lake, crying like plovers. They never came back. It was bedlam, and when I looked in my telescope the dog star was raging to the west.

CLEMMY: I've always hated the place.

CLARRY: Mukinupin?

CLEMMY: Exiled here like shags on rocks.

CLARRY: I know you've missed it, Clemmy, but who wouldn't? Up there in the Big Top with the crowd holding their breaths.

CLEMMY: I could see the five Wirth sisters playing at statues on their powdered horses, looking up, everybody looking up… and then… suddenly…

She covers her face with her hands.

ZEEK: Moons rise, stars fall…

CLARRY: Don't brood on it, dear. It's such a long time ago.

CLEMMY: I'm like a bird with a broken wing.

On the soundtrack the night sounds begin.

CLARRY: [*sleepily*] Who's that giggling in the creek bed?

CLEMMY: Touch of the Tar.

CLARRY: [*murmuring*] I can hear a madman screaming.

CLEMMY: It's only the Flasher, tuning into Marconi.

They giggle. Pause.

CLARRY: I think I can hear a willie wagtail. Listen, Clem, [*murmuring*] sweet pretty creature... sweet pretty creature.

Her voice dies away.

CLEMMY: I couldn't dance much, y'know Clarry, I couldn't really hit a high C, and my legs were terrible, but by God... I could walk that highwire. [*Pause.*] Goodnight, Clarry. Sweet dreams.

The MISSES HUMMER *sleep.*

ZEEK: And certain stars shot madly from their spheres flying between the cold moon and the earth.

The night sounds fill the stage. Enter HARRY TUESDAY, *ready for the road, with rifle, bandolier and swag, wearing a Digger's hat. He sits and rolls a smoke, dropping his swag at his feet.*

How goes the night, boy?

'NEW HOLLAND SONG'

HARRY: New Holland is a barren place,
          In it there grows no grain,
          Nor any habitation
          Wherein for to remain.

          She is my gold, my darling,
          She gives me drought and rain,
          When I plough and sow her
          Upon the saltbush plain,

          She is my bitter heritage,
          She is my darling one,
          She drowns me in the winter
          And she bakes me in the sun.

          I'll plant her and I'll rape her,
          I will not run her down,
          Upon her gold and torment
          I'll build my shanty town,

          Cut her plains with sheep pads,
          Mine the black beach sand,
          Push the iron ranges down

And salt the Great South Land.

And then she will repay me,
For she will give no grain,
Nor any habitation
Wherein for to remain.

HARRY *picks up his swag and moves off, singing. During the song* ZEEK *has been packing up his telescope.*

ZEEK: The moon shines with a good grace. Well shone, Moon.

He takes his divining rod, moves along stage front, places a stone in the place of greatest pull, and measures foot to foot along the stage. He pauses and turns centre.

[*Triumphantly*] Dig here. You'll get water at sixty feet.

The shadowy figure of ZEEK is left, centre stage, holding his divining rod like a prophet.

END OF ACT ONE

ACT TWO

The stage is empty and set exactly the same as in Act One. The time is 1918. A steam train can be heard approaching in the distance, a train whistle blows 'Yankee Doodle Dandy' insistently several times like a signal. Enter the townspeople in various stages of early morning undress: the HUMMER SISTERS *yawning in dressing-gowns,* EDIE PERKINS *in hair curlers,* EEK *still in shirtsleeves, with lather on his face and a cut-throat razor in his hand.* CECIL BRUNNER *has forgotten his toupée. They stand about bewildered and exclaiming to each other:*

ALL: What is it? Did you hear the train? Playing a tune. 'Yankee Doodle Dandy'!

> EEK *comes centre stage. He holds up his hand.*

EEK: Hark!

> *They all stand silently listening. The train whistle repeats the refrain. Enter* POLLY PERKINS *running on, wild with excitement, dressed in a white blouse, black skirt and button-up boots, waving a telegram.*

POLLY: The war's over. It just came through on the wire.

> *The town crowd around* POLLY, *calling out…*

VARIOUS: When? What happened? Tell us, Polly. What's she saying?

> POLLY *unfolds the telegram importantly, and comes centre stage.*

POLLY: [*reading*] 'London, November the eleventh, 1918, ten fifty-five a.m., most urgent. Armistice signed at five o'clock this morning.'

EEK: [*reverently*] Ah! The wonders of modern science.

CLEMMY: [*wryly*] Even in Mukinupin.

POLLY: [*softly*] Jack will be coming home.

> EDIE *runs up and down with her ear trumpet.*

EDIE: What she say, what she say? Speak up, Pol, do.

EEK: [*roaring*] War's over!

ALL: War's over! War's over! War's over!

> *They move in a ritual circle, shaking hands, smiling, exclaiming.* CECIL, *embarrassed, suddenly remembers his toupée, adjusts it*

hurriedly, and kisses the ladies' hands. When he reaches POLLY *she ignores him, remaining apart in a dream of* JACK *as the train plays 'Yankee Doodle Dandy' and the church bells ring out. They all sing a wartime medley beginning with 'Yankee Doodle' and moving into one or two of the following: 'Keep the Home Fires Burning', 'Tipperary', 'Take Me Back to Dear Old Blighty', or 'Pack Up Your Troubles'. During the songs* EEK *and* CECIL *exit and bring back a huge boomerang of flower. The* HUMMER SISTERS *exit, then return dressed in their best, carrying a floral star five feet across.* EDIE *takes the curlers out of her hair;* POLLY *primps in a hand mirror;* EEK *wipes the lather off his face, and as the train hisses and whistles and they move into the solemn tones of the Recessional,* EDIE *and* POLLY *produce a bunting sign with 'WELCOME HOME MUKINUPIN'S HERO'.*

Enter JACK TUESDAY, *in Digger's uniform, carrying his kitbag and looking bewildered. They all crowd around, singing their lungs out, while* JACK *stands centre stage, surrounded by floral tributes.* CECIL *and* EEK *carry* JACK *shoulder-high along the street, with the others following. They place him on the table top, pile the flowers around him, still singing.* EEK *holds up his hand for silence and reads his speech from the Town Hall steps.*

EEK: Fellow citizens, I feel I stand here today in the reflected glory of the Australian soldier.

Loud cheers from everybody except the embarrassed JACK.

After five years of the most dreaded war the world has ever known; the fearful horrors of trench warfare, a Europe drenched in gore; we stand here to welcome home our returning hero... [*He brandishes his cut-throat razor.*] It is true that not the faintest breath of these horrors ravaged our fair young shores, but we gave our sons to face the test of manhood, and, in the grey light of early dawn, leap out upon unknown shores to dare, endure and die.

Cries and sobs from the crowd. JACK *hangs his head.*

Yes, Australia was there, and Mukinupin was there, to crush Germany and re-divide the world. At one stride our young Commonwealth put on the toga of nationhood, vindicated the rights of man, and maintained the moral order of the universe. Let us pray.

Still fiercely brandishing his razor EEK *falls on his knees and begins the Lord's Prayer.* JACK *hesitates but follows. They all join in, except* EDIE, *who, sublimely unknowing, begins to recite.*

EDIE: The bugles of the Motherland
    Rang ceaselessly across the sea,
    To call him and his lean brown band
    To shape Imperial destiny;
    He went by youth's grave purpose willed,
    The goal unknown, the cost outweighed,
    The promise of his blood fulfilled—
EEK: [*furious*] Will you hold your tongue, Mother.
EDIE: [*crossly*] The bravest thing God ever made.

They all break into 'Mademoiselle from Armentières'. JACK *grins and they all, except* EEK, *rise and circle* JACK, *hand in hand, singing.*

ALL: Speech, speech.
JACK: [*embarrassed*] I'm glad to be back—and still alive.

Hoorays, coo-ees.

POLLY: [*with pride*] My Jack's a hero.
JACK: No, Pol, I'm not. You've got it all wrong. Harry.

Dead silence.

ALL: [*amazed*] Harry!
JACK: That's right. Harry got the VC at Hill 60—for extraordinary gallantry—under fire. There was nobody left in 'is bloody platoon.
ALL: No!
JACK: [*cheerfully*] Harry always was a wild bugger. So you see, you got the wrong snoozer. Can I get down now?

    EEK *rises from his knees.*

EEK: This is most embarrassing, Jack Tuesday.
JACK: Yeah, I know, it is a bit of a bummer. Mind you, I'm still not as embarrassin' as Harry.
EEK: Where is… Harry?
JACK: Jumped ship at Albany, deserted and went bush. But I would'nt bother about gettin' out the red carpet for Harry. He's shell-shocked, off his chump, takes fits and dribbles. Balmy Harry, they calls 'im.

POLLY *runs forward and clasps* JACK *in her arms.*

POLLY: Well, I don't care anyway. I'm just glad you're back, safe and sound.

CLARRY & CLEMMY: Hear, hear!

JACK: [*grinning*] Me too. Jeez, Pol, you look good enough to eat.

JACK *hugs* POLLY.

POLLY: I missed you, Jack. You only wrote twice.

JACK: Ah! Well, you know I was never much of a hand with the pen.

EDIE: What's he say?

EEK: [*bawling*] He's not a hero... or much of a hand with the pen!

EDIE: I might have known it.

Disgusted, she rolls up the bunting.

EEK: Well, Jack, we won't hold this against you. Even if you're not a hero.

CECIL: No, indeed.

EEK: You did your bit and now we're prepared to do ours.

But JACK *has been canoodling with* POLLY, *much to* CECIL'*s chagrin, and doesn't take much notice.* EEK *clears his throat.*

Jack Tuesday, I'm prepared to offer you your old job back again in Perkins' General Store. I'll always support a trier.

EDIE *holds out the broom for* JACK *to take.*

JACK: I'll die laughin'.

CECIL: You could do worse, Jack. Mukinupin's quite the little metropolis.

EEK: Work hard, produce plenty and pay your debts, that's Mukinupin.

CLARRY: We're just one big happy family in Mucka.

POLLY: Father shaves in a silver mug and Mother [*giggling*] uses a Royal Doulton chamber pot with forget-me-nots round the rim.

EEK: Some of you doubted, but I never doubted.

POLLY: And oh, Jack, guess what! I've got a vieux rose bedroom, with a big clock going tick-tock-tick on the landing.

JACK: I don't want to be a grocer's boy in Perkins' General Store.

POLLY: Oh, Jack.

EEK: I can understand that.

CECIL: Oh, perfectly understandable.

EEK: I'll make another offer. What about… the land?

JACK: Ma's dead of gallopin' consumption, so you can keep the lousy farm. It's only stinkwort and poison bush anyway.

POLLY: Oh, Jack, you'll never get on.

JACK: Get on! Be a farm labourer, workin' sun-up till dark six days a week, live in a tin shed with a stretcher in it for a quid a week and me keep. Come off it, Pol. No, I'm goin' shearin'.

EEK & CECIL: With the red-raggers and no-hopers.

>EEK *exits, disgusted, with* CECIL. EDIE *and the* HUMMER SISTERS *gather up the floral tributes and exit.*

POLLY: Oh, Jack, I've waited so long for you to come home. Ever since that last night when we quarrelled. You never even spent your last night in Mukinupin with me.

JACK: [*uneasy*] I know, Pol.

POLLY: Where did you spend it, then?

JACK: I got shickered.

POLLY: [*disgusted*] Somebody said you were with Touch of the Tar.

JACK: Did they?

POLLY: Well, were you?

>*As* JACK *and* POLLY *confront each other,* EEK *and* CECIL *re-enter with ladder and bunting, and put up a large sign in front of the Mukinupin Town Hall. It reads 'LEST WE FORGET'. The* MISSES HUMMER *enter, staggering under a cardboard statue of a soldier with a kelpie dog at his feet.* EDIE *follows with a bunch of flowers. They set it all in place and when they have all finished their respective jobs they exit.*

JACK: Ask no questions and you'll hear no lies.

>POLLY *turns her back on him.*

POLLY: Go shearing, then—see if I care.

JACK: I'm only back two minutes, and you're at me again.

POLLY: I hate you, Jack Tuesday.

JACK: No you don't, Pol.

>JACK *comes behind her and clasps her waist, kissing her ear.*

POLLY: I thought it would be so lovely, just you and me, like it used to be, behind the dust on the counters.

JACK: Nothin's changed, Pol.

POLLY: Everything's changed, but you've changed most of all.

JACK: I've grown up, that's all. I've seen the world, Pol. I've got to live me own life, and you've got to let me.

POLLY: And what about my life? How can I marry… a shearer?

JACK: [*teasing*] No vieux rose bedroom, no silver shavin' mug or forget-me-not jerry.

POLLY: I think I'll marry Cecil Brunner. He's got a position.

JACK: You'll never marry him.

POLLY: You better watch out, Jack Tuesday, because, if you treat me badly, I just might, y' know.

JACK: Don't threaten me, Polly.

He catches her waist.

I don't treat you badly, do I? Do I?

POLLY: It's too long ago. I don't remember.

JACK *pulls her towards him. She struggles but, when he kisses her, she responds.* POLLY *breaks away.*

Ah Jack! You make it so hard for me.

JACK: I won't be shearin' forever. It's only a stopgap. I'll make it—one a' these days.

POLLY: Make it, how?

JACK: I dunno. I just know—I will, and then we can be married and you can go on bein' the lady.

POLLY: I don't believe you.

JACK: I tell you it's true. I'll be a… a…

A long pause.

POLLY: You'll be a what?

JACK: I'll be an… actor, that's what I'll be. I'll be an actor, Pol.

POLLY: [*scornfully*] An actor?

JACK: That's right. Remember the Montebellos?

POLLY: That old woman who made sheep's eyes at you?

JACK: Remember how impressed they were?

POLLY: I remember how she buttered you up, that's all. He wasn't impressed.

JACK: He was jealous. He could see… another performer in the offing.

POLLY: You're impossible. [*She turns away.*] It's all dreams, Jack, just
pipe dreams.

JACK: You don't believe in me, that's your trouble. You just don't
believe in me at all.

POLLY *exits and* JACK *comes centre stage for his song.*

'FLASH JACK OF MUKINUPIN'

I trudged beyond Jitarning Soak,
I passed the Kunjin plain,
I left behind the rabbit-proof,
Wet wool and drizzlin' rain,

In mud and blood in Flanders' fields
The whizz-bangs were all poppin',
Flash Jack survived with his nine lives,
Come back to Mukinupin.

Chorus:

Tumble in their beds, boys,
Skirts above their heads, boys,
I can do a respectable tally meself,
I take a lot of stoppin',
And they know me round the backblocks
As Flash Jack from Mukinupin.

And it's all around the country,
In me moleskins and me hat,
I'm the latest kind of flasher
Out on the One Tree Flat.

At Kunna and at Mucka
I will kiss the girls and then
I'll call in at the shanty
And say fill 'em up again.

Repeat chorus:

And all the girls in Mucka
Will take a shine to me,
I'll love 'em and I'll leave 'em
Underneath the pepper tree,

Before me time is all cut out,
And I've called it a day,
I'll have every girl in Mucka
In the family way.

Repeat chorus:

JACK *dances towards the war memorial, takes out a cigarette, lights it and seats himself at the foot of the memorial. Enter* MERCY MONTEBELLO, *carrying a hatbox and suitcase and dressed in the height of fashion. She has just come off the train. With languid grace she removes her gloves and hat, and gazes around her with undisguised loathing. She goes to the mirror to fix her hair then runs her finger over the furniture.*

MERCY: Mukinupin, Mukinupin. Hasn't changed a jot in five long years; dust still as thick, silence still as deep, flyspots still as various. Ah! Max, Max. [*She sits, holding her head in her hands in a Victorian pose.*] Your Mercy has fallen upon evil days. [*She pulls herself together, takes up writing paper and pen.*] But nil desperandum, as the Greek philosopher says; Mercy Montebello can still make a silk purse out of a sow's ear. [*She gazes out front for inspiration, sucking her pen.*] Dearest Jack… no, that won't do. Dear Jack—too formal. My dear Jack… that's better… My dear Jack, I arrived by train this morning and thought I might in remembrance of older and happier times… just… drop you this line…

She rises, essaying a few graceful dance steps as she speaks the following dialogue to music.

Do you remember the old times?
I remember too well,
I've been waiting all morning
In a suite at the Royal Hotel.

I've come to Mucka by train, Jack,
Desdemona is free.
Max collapsed into the footlights
Whilst he was strangling me.

Don't hope to see a beauty,
I'm just a faded rose,

But I'd like to take your hand, Jack,
Before I take my repose.

She sits for the last lines of her letter.

I haven't any designs, dear,
Cross my heart, hope to die,
But I'll wear a hat with a feather,
And you wear a spotted tie.

I recall when we met, Jack,
The wheat was a burnished yellow,
We were innocent, young, then;
Love, Mercy Montebello.

She places the letter in an envelope and firmly licks the flap.

That should bring him running.

Enter CECIL BRUNNER *in bowler hat, carrying a huge bunch of long-stemmed pink roses. He bows over* MERCY's *hand.* MERCY *rises.*

CECIL: [*stuttering*] Welcome, Madame Montebello. What an honour... our little town... [*et cetera*]

MERCY: So charming of you, Mr... Mr...?

CECIL: Brunner, but please call me Cecil.

MERCY: I wouldn't presume.

CECIL: The presumption is all on my part, Madame.

MERCY: [*aside*] It is rather, but how can I make use of his presumption...? [*To* CECIL] Mr Brunner... Cecil... your roses are exquisite.

She takes them.

CECIL: They do not come within coo-ee of your unearthly beauty, Madame.

MERCY: Within coo-ee. What an odd expression. Is that local dialect?

CECIL: I fear so, Madame. I am, after all, only a humble colonial.

MERCY: A humble man may dare where others fail. What is your calling, pray?

CECIL: I travel, Madame.

MERCY: Travel, travel where? Are you a strolling player, one of our fraternity?

CECIL: A knight of the road, certainly, but I travel in ladies' lingerie.

MERCY: [*shocked*] An underwear salesman!

CECIL: You could... describe me as such.

MERCY: If you have come to make a sale, I assure you... the cupboard is bare.

CECIL: [*with dignity*] I come only as a sincere admirer, Madame.

MERCY: Do you happen to know a Mr Jack Tuesday? Is he still in the district?

CECIL: I have that doubtful privilege. Jack Tuesday has just returned from the war.

MERCY: Covered in glory, no doubt.

CECIL: [*bitterly*] Masquerading as some sort of hero.

MERCY: I am seeking Mr Tuesday, because I think he may be able to repair my fading fortunes.

CECIL: Jack?

MERCY: He is handsome, well set-up, has a pleasant singing voice, can dance nimbly, and has something of a presence. In short, with my assistance he could make a career for himself on the boards.

CECIL: Jack... an actor?

MERCY: Trust in me, my experience, Mr... er... Cecil. It is not inconsiderable.

CECIL: [*thoughtfully*] You would take him away from here?

MERCY: Certainement. You could hardly make a career in the Mukinupin Town Hall. [*She shudders and takes up her letter.*] I have written him a letter asking him to meet me here. [*Pause.*] He had, I think... some species of... fiancée?

CECIL: Polly, but they're not really engaged. Only she...

MERCY: Fancies him, well, what female would'nt? That's my point. He'd make such a divine Dandino.

CECIL: [*gloomily*] Would he?

MERCY: You have some aspirations in Polly's direction yourself?

CECIL: I did have, but begin to despair.

    MERCY *claps him on the shoulder.*

MERCY: Take heart, sir. Deliver my message and your troubles are probably over.

CECIL: Do you really think so?

    He takes the letter.

Oh, Madame, if it were only true.

MERCY: Come, who could resist Mercy Montebello?

She sashays around the room.

CECIL: Who indeed!

He bows low over her hand again.

MERCY: Fly, Mr Cecil. You are, indeed, the messenger of fortune.

He moves off. MERCY *puts up her hand.*

Mr Cecil.

He pauses.

Could you, would you, lend me my fare out of town?

CECIL: Certainly, Madame.

He fumbles in his pocket and hands her the money with a bow.

MERCY: God will reward you, for it's pretty certain Mercy Montebello cannot.

She kisses his cheek. He presses his hand to his blushing cheek and stumbles out, in a daze.

God speed, Mr Cecil.

She moves across to the glass and begins making up. CECIL *crosses to* JACK, *elaborately casual.*

CECIL: Evenin', Jack.

JACK: Evenin'.

CECIL: Bit on the gloomy side?

No answer.

I've a message for you. Every cloud has a silver lining.

JACK: From Polly?

CECIL: From Mercy Montebello.

JACK *leaps up.*

JACK: Mercy… in town?

He grabs the letter and begins to read.

CECIL: At the Royal… somewhat down on her luck.

JACK: She wants to see me, and I'm to wear… a spotted bow tie. [*He looks worried.*] I haven't got one.

CECIL: Feel free.

He unties his own spotted tie and hands it to JACK, *who knots it untidily around his neck.*

JACK: How do I look?

CECIL: [*dryly*] Magnificent!

JACK starts to move across the stage. He stops.

JACK: Is she still… as… beautiful?

CECIL: As a gazelle—if a little long in the tooth.

JACK *grins.*

JACK: Thanks, Cec. I'll do as much for you some day.

CECIL *exits.* MERCY *stands, looking nervous.* JACK *stands, looking nervous.*

Mercy… it's me. Jack. I got your letter.

MERCY *dabs at her eyes with a handkerchief.*

MERCY: [*tearfully*] Oh, Jack!

JACK: [*clumsily*] Don't cry, Merc. I'll look after you.

MERCY *lays her head on his shoulder.*

MERCY: Dear Jack. Still as handsome as ever, and as kind.

JACK: [*gallantly*] And you're still as beautiful.

MERCY: You recognised me?

JACK: Who could ever forget… Mercy Montebello.

MERCY: The world apparently. Ah! Jack, Jack, the public are so fickle. Since Max… passed away.

She sobs a little.

JACK: Don't talk about it… please.

MERCY: I've had no-one to turn to. A woman alone is [*gesturing*]…

JACK: Turn to me.

MERCY: What gallantry… my dear.

JACK: Any bloke would envy me, Merc.

MERCY: Let me fix your tie…

She does so, very provocatively. Their eyes meet.

There, that's better.

She sways away, sits and takes a flask of gin out of her purse.

Have a spot, Jack.

JACK: Don't mind if I do.

She fills two glasses and hands one to JACK.

MERCY: To us.

They drink.

And now—down to business.

JACK: Business?

MERCY *tinkles with laughter.*

MERCY: Don't get the wrong idea, Jack. This is—strictly a business proposition. [*She makes outrageous eyes at him.*] I thought you understood that.

JACK: Oh!

MERCY: Come, Jack. I'm old enough to be your ma.

JACK: [*gloomily*] I 'spect you are.

MERCY: But that doesn't stop us having a great deal to give each other.

JACK: [*cheering up*] You reckon?

MERCY: I reckon; so listen carefully to what I have to say.

JACK *nods and leans forward in his chair.*

I'm looking for a new partner. I can't work alone. I need a foil, with masculine bravado to offset my... womanly tenderness. Anyway, I'm thinking of leaving the classics and moving into something more picturesque and tuneful, with exotique settings and catchy songs... something with a genuine appeal to the romantic longings of our audiences. You follow me?

JACK *nods violently.*

And that, dear Jack, is where you come in.

JACK: [*stupidly*] Where do I come in?

MERCY: [*gaily*] I'm asking you to be my partner in this enterprise.

JACK: Why me?

MERCY: Look at you.

She pulls him to his feet and twirls him around.

You have such grace, such charm, such... élan. Every woman in the audience will fall in love with you. In short, dear Jack, you have the sex appeal.

JACK: Have I?

MERCY *laughs at him.*

'MERCY AND JACK'S DUET'

MERCY: Oh! Would you like to sing
         A short duet with me?
         I wouldn't ask for more than this.
JACK: I'll be laconic,
MERCY: Strictly platonic,
JACK & MERCY: Let's seal it with a kiss.
MERCY: Oh! Jack, we're going places,
         In silks and laces,
         We'll know how far to go,
         We'll give them a show, a dream,
         They've never seen a show like ours before.
JACK & MERCY: We'll stop in all the best hotels,
         When we step out they'll ring the bells.
MERCY: You'll order cocktails,
         I'll dress up to kill,
JACK & MERCY: And up in lights we'll have
         Our double bill.
MERCY: We'll be seen in all the chic
         And stylish places,
JACK: You'll take my arm,
         We'll have such charm,
MERCY: Élan.
JACK & MERCY: We'll have our faces in the magazines.
         So would you like to sing
         A short duet with me?
         I wouldn't ask for more than this,
JACK: I'll be laconic,
MERCY: Strictly platonic,
JACK & MERCY: Let's seal it with a kiss,
         With a kiss.

         They kiss, but MERCY *breaks away.*

MERCY: The only problem is—will you take my offer seriously?
JACK: Oh, I will, I will.
MERCY: What plans have you for your future?

JACK: No plans. Oh well, I was thinkin' of goin' shearin'. But of course I'd drop all that like a hot potater.

MERCY: But what about your little friend... little Miss Whatsisname... Polly?

JACK: Polly'll be delighted. She wants me to get on.

MERCY: She may not want to lose you.

JACK: That's true. [*Pause.*] I don't suppose, Miss Mercy, we could find a place for Pol?

MERCY: I wonder. [*She drums on the table with her fingers.*] I don't really see why not. She's a pretty little thing... front of house, perhaps.

JACK: Oh, Merc, you're such a brick. If we could only take Pol I'd be the happiest man on earth.

MERCY: Then it's decided. I won't even unpack. We'll leave on the train this evening. Have you got your fare?

JACK: Too right. I've got me deferred pay.

MERCY: Capital! Now where can we find your Polly?

JACK: She'll be in a vieux rose bedroom with a clock ticking on the landing, dreaming of being a lady.

MERCY: In Mukinupin! Poor thing. Well then, Jack my dear, let us go and change your Polly's life.

> JACK *picks up* MERCY*'s bags while she puts on her hat and fixes it before the mirror. They move off together and* JACK *raps loudly on the counter.*

JACK: Pol, are you there?

> *Enter* POLLY *dressed to the nines.*

POLLY: [*sweetly*] Yes, Jack.

JACK: [*awkwardly*] Polly, you remember Miss—Madame Montebello.

POLLY: Oh, I do. You're looking very well, Madame.

MERCY: Thank you, Polly.

JACK: Madame has a... proposition to make.

POLLY: Please do sit down.

> *They do so, very stiffly.*

A proposition?

JACK: Yes, a business proposition.

POLLY: Indeed?

JACK: And it includes you. Oh, Pol, please say yes, it means the whole world… to both of us.

POLLY: What is… this business proposition?

MERCY: In short, Miss Polly, my husband is dead and I am looking for a partner.

POLLY *gives a horrified gasp.*

[*Patiently*] A business partner. I need a principal man.

POLLY: But Jack's a grocer's boy.

JACK: [*grimly*] Not anymore I'm not.

MERCY: We all have to be discovered—somewhere.

POLLY: In Mukinupin?

MERCY: Even in Mukinupin. You must not stand in his way, my dear. Your Jack has talent—and charm. He's wasted in these… desert places.

POLLY: [*wailing*] So you're taking him away.

JACK *takes her hand.*

JACK: No, Polly, listen. Madame Montebello—Mercy wants you too.

POLLY: For what? A bit of window dressing?

JACK: [*bitterly*] Spoken like a true Perkins. Polly, the drapers' daughter!

MERCY: You could be very useful to us, Polly. Front of house, public relations, who knows? You could play it by ear.

POLLY: It doesn't appeal to me, Madame.

JACK: But why not, why not?

POLLY: Just because…

JACK *leaps up, grabs her shoulders and shakes her.*

JACK: Because what? Don't play games with me, Polly Perkins.

POLLY *starts to cry.*

POLLY: Because I won't be used: that's why, Jack Tuesday. [*To* MERCY] Oh, you think you can pull the wool over my eyes, you and your fine feathers. I can see right through you. It's Jack you're after, always has been. You and your business arrangements!

MERCY: I beg your pardon?

JACK: How dare you speak to Madame Montebello in that tone of voice. Apologise!

POLLY: I won't, I won't.

JACK: Apologise!

POLLY: I'm a nice girl.

JACK: Not nice enough.

POLLY: You'd be in clover, Jack, wouldn't you, with the two of us? You could switch around.

> JACK *slaps her face. She runs crying offstage. A long pause as* JACK *shakily lights a cigarette.*

MERCY: [*quietly*] Well, Jack, it won't work, will it?

JACK: [*miserably*] I could come with you anyway.

MERCY: But I don't think you will.

JACK: Oh, Merc, I don't know what to do.

MERCY: If you make up your mind, I'll be at the station waiting for the train out of Mukinupin. Au revoir, Jack.

> JACK *moves across to her.*

JACK: Thank you for asking me.

MERCY: The offer's open—always, Jack.

> *She lifts up her face for a kiss. They kiss gently, then passionately.*

You kiss—so passionately.

JACK: [*breathless*] So do you.

> MERCY *moves across and picks up her bags.*

Let me carry your bags.

MERCY: I can manage. I'm an independent woman.

> *She exits.* JACK *sits at the table. He takes two bottles of beer out of his knapsack and puts them down belligerently. Enter* CECIL BRUNNER. JACK *loosens his tie and tears it off.*

JACK: You can take your bloody tie.

CECIL: What's up, Jack?

JACK: [*mimicking him*] What's up, Jack? I'll tell what's up—all hell and damnation, that's what's up.

> CECIL *sits opposite him.*

CECIL: It can't be as bad as that.

JACK: Can't it? [*He looks at* CECIL *suspiciously.*] Now I come to think of it, how was it that you delivered that note from Mercy Montebello?

CECIL: I was just passing by.

JACK: [*drinking heavily*] Oh, yeah.

CECIL: And Madame Montebello asked me to deliver her letter. [*He pauses defensively.*] I've always admired her. She's a very fine figure of a woman.

JACK: [*savagely*] Like you've admired Polly. [*He leans across the table.*] Listen, Brunner, if I thought that you deliberately set me up...

CECIL: I don't know what you're suggesting.

JACK: I bet. You've always wanted Polly, since she was a little bit of a kid. Well, haven't you?

CECIL: [*stiffly*] I love Miss Polly—yes, it's true.

JACK: And you thought if you got me out of the way you'd have a better chance? All's fair in love and war.

CECIL: I want to marry her.

JACK: Well, maybe now you'll get your wish. How does that affect you?

CECIL: I'll always be here if she needs me.

JACK: After all, you're more her type... [*with scorn*] a travelling salesman.

CECIL: [*with dignity*] There are worse things.

JACK: You reckon?

CECIL: I'd give her... security.

JACK: That's what she wants, alright. Okay, Cec, you're on your own, by Christ, and I hope you make it. [*He rises, swaying noticeably.*] The Perkinses'll be pleased, and Pol'll be a lady. It's what she's always wanted, and no hard feelin's.

> JACK *claps* CECIL *on the shoulders and lurches over to the war memorial where he sits drinking. Enter* EDIE *behind the counter.* CECIL *crosses to her and begins unpacking his sample case.*

CECIL: I've got some lovely stuff for the summer trade, Mrs Perkins.

EDIE: You always have such good taste, Mr Brunner.

> CECIL *begins displaying his wares.*

CECIL: This trousseau set's a real stunner.

EDIE: [*coyly*] I'd like to see our Polly modelling that.

> *During the following scene* CECIL *exits.*

JACK: [*singing*] Polly lies over the ocean,

Polly lies over the sea,
Polly lies over the ocean,
O bring back my Polly to me.
Bring back, bring back,
O bring back my Polly to me.

Enter TOUCH OF THE TAR *in her ragged dress, barefoot. She sidles up to* JACK.

TOUCH OF THE TAR: It's Jack Toosday, isn't it?
JACK: [*sulkily*] Y'know it is.

She sits beside him.

TOUCH OF THE TAR: Could never mistake yous. You an' 'Arry.
JACK: Everybody does.
TOUCH OF THE TAR: You're diff'rent. [*Giggling*] I oughta know.

She leans her head against JACK's *knee.*

I like you, Jackie.
JACK: Good luck, Lily.
TOUCH OF THE TAR: Don' you talk to me like that. Why you talk about luck ter me?
JACK: Because you need it. You an' me both. Here, take a swig.

TOUCH OF THE TAR *drinks heavily. They share the bottle.*

TOUCH OF THE TAR: Me bastard farver come from Mucka.
JACK: I know.
TOUCH OF THE TAR: I'm not a prostitute… no way. I just hates men.
JACK: You don't hate me.
TOUCH OF THE TAR: Why not?
JACK: Because I never hurt you.
TOUCH OF THE TAR: Why do I like you?
JACK: Because we're both… outcasts.
TOUCH OF THE TAR: Why doncha get off with me agen?
JACK: It wouldn't be any good in the mornin'.
TOUCH OF THE TAR: I'm not good enough for you. Thass it.
JACK: For either of us.
TOUCH OF THE TAR: Then give us two bob, will y'?
JACK: Don't talk to me like that.
TOUCH OF THE TAR: Ah, I don't give a fuck, anyway. I'm tired of it,

hangin' about on the edge of town, treated like shit.

JACK: You an' me both, Lil.

TOUCH OF THE TAR: Let's go then, Jackie.

JACK: You're Harry's girl.

TOUCH OF THE TAR: I'm nobody's. Come on, take a real good look at me, in the daylight. I'm nobody's, but I'm pretty, ain't I?

JACK: Yeah, you are.

TOUCH OF THE TAR: Then let's piss off, Jackie, you an' me. You could do a lot worse.

JACK: You really want to go?

TOUCH OF THE TAR: Too right. What's keepin' us here?

JACK: You couldn't go like that.

> TOUCH OF THE TAR *stiffens.*

TOUCH OF THE TAR: What's wrong with me?

JACK: You look like a tramp.

TOUCH OF THE TAR: Ah shit, you're jus' like all the rest—white men.

> *She takes another swig.* JACK *stands up, swaying slightly, and pulls her to her feet.*

JACK: No, if you go with me, you'll go like a lady. You're pretty an' you're nice and you'll go like a lady. D'ya hear?

TOUCH OF THE TAR: [*sulkily*] Go where?

JACK: Everywhere; the whole wide world, maybe. You an' me and Madame Montebello.

TOUCH OF THE TAR: She wouldn't want me. She's a stuck-up bitch, I bet.

JACK: No she's not. She's an actress. Maybe you could be one, too.

TOUCH OF THE TAR: Me?

> *She laughs incredulously.*

JACK: Get some decent clobber on you and you'd be a knock out, Lil. Come on.

> JACK *begins dragging her in the direction of Perkins' store, but she hangs back.*

TOUCH OF THE TAR: Where we goin'?

JACK: To buy you a new dress and a pair of shoes and a hat and—

TOUCH OF THE TAR: I'm not goin' in there.

JACK: You're comin' with me.

TOUCH OF THE TAR: That bitch won't serve me.

> JACK *drags her across the stage to* EDIE PERKINS.

JACK: We need a dress, and shoes, and a hat, everythin' to fit.

EDIE: What's that?

JACK: You heard. [*He roars into her ear trumpet.*] Dress. Hat. Shoes.

EDIE: We don't serve blacks in here.

> JACK *pounds on the counter.*

JACK: You're servin' me. Get it. Me! Now… Dress, hat, shoes and the best—none of your rubbish. I want somethin' like—somethin' like Polly'd wear.

EDIE: [*faintly*] Polly would wear.

JACK: Get it.

> *As* EDIE *brings out a white muslin dress with sash, a big picture hat and black pumps with bows* TOUCH OF THE TAR *exclaims with delight. She peels off her dress, tries on the new clothes and dances about the room.*

TOUCH OF THE TAR: Jesus, Jack! Look at this. Oh! Ain't it just lovely?

JACK: And I want a parasol.

> *Enter the two* MISSES HUMMER*;* CLARRY *with her sewing basket and* CLEMMY *leaning on her stick. They sit in their armchairs.* CLARRY *takes out her sewing,* CLEMMY *fans herself with her sandalwood fan.* JACK *pays* EDIE.

CLEMMY: It's a scorcher.

CLARRY: A hundred and fourteen in the shade.

CLEMMY: Drought and rabbits.

CLARRY: Rabbits and drought.

CLEMMY: Looks like the end of the world, dear.

CLARRY: Salt's rising.

CLEMMY: Soak's gone bitter.

CLARRY: Honeysuckle's dying.

CLEMMY: Even the birds are dropping out of the sky.

CLARRY: And the tanks are empty. We'll have to start carting soon.

CLEMMY & CLARRY: No good for the crops.

> *Exit* JACK *and* TOUCH OF THE TAR. EDIE *starts to sob. Enter* EEK

PERKINS *with his paper. He sits in the armchair, ignoring* EDIE.

CLARRY: There's that myall girl, Touch of the Tar, sashaying down to the siding, dressed up to kill.

CLEMMY: Lily Perkins!

CLARRY: Leaving town.

CLEMMY: With Jack Tuesday.

CLARRY: Poor Polly.

CLEMMY: Polly's lying down in the best bedroom with eau de cologne on her hankie.

CLARRY: Listening to Galli Curci on the phonograph.

CLEMMY: [*giggling*] Singing 'My Tiny Hand Is Frozen'.

CLARRY: She's always been the little lady.

CLEMMY: And a bit too big for her boots.

EDIE: I was a refined and cultured woman, Mr Perkins, before you brought me to this sink of Sodom.

EEK: Town's like an oven.

EDIE: Dressing up a black gin to look like our Polly.

EEK: Ninety-seven enlisted men and twenty-four died. Not a bad record for Mucka.

The light begins to fade as HARRY TUESDAY *enters in ragged moleskins, a black singlet, a slouch hat, bare feet and drinking a bottle of beer. He is already very drunk. He sits at the foot of the war memorial.*

CLARRY: [*whispering*] There's Harry Tuesday.

HARRY: I was awarded a VC an' two bars for givin' a corp. a kick in the arse.

He chuckles wildly.

CLEMMY: Harry's back home.

CLARRY: It's a wonder he's saved his neck this long.

HARRY *begins to sing drunkenly.*

HARRY: [*singing*] I wanta go home,
    I wanta go home,
    I don't wanta go to the trenches no more,
    Where hand grenades an' whizz-bangs they roar.
[*Speaking*] I'm shickered, an' may the best man win.

EDIE: I never speak, I cannot speak of these matters, without I... choke with emotion.

EEK: The Albany doctor'll be blowing up soon.

HARRY: [*singing*] So send me over the sea,
    Where the Heinies can't get at me,
    O my, I'm too young ter die,
    I wanta go home.

EDIE: Lowest creatures on God's earth. They're all only animals... animals...

HARRY: And there was nobody left in the whole bloody platoon.

He collapses, laughing again.

EDIE: Well, I hope she's gone for good, that's all. I hope she's gone for good. [*Firmly*] Because I tell you, Eek Perkins, I've never been so humiliated—serving your bastard.

EEK *drops his paper and stares at her. There is a long pause. He picks it up again.*

EEK: Wheat's up seven and fourpence ha'penny a bushel.

Long pause. EDIE *stares hiccupping into the night;* EEK *reads his paper.*

The only way you can teach a nigger is with a big stick.

CLARRY *sews,* CLEMMY *fans herself, as* HARRY *continues to sing into the darkness.*

HARRY: Where whiz-bangs are flyin' and brave men are dyin'
    For bastards like you, dinky-di, dinky-bloody-die,
    Dinky-die, dinky-di, dinky-di.
    Dinky-bloody-di...

HARRY *moves off, singing and taking a swig from his bottle, as the lights come up on* POLLY *entering with bolts of material.* POLLY, CLARRY *and* CLEMMY *make a semi-circle sewing bee;* EEK *changes his paper for the earphones of a crystal set.* POLLY *begins sewing.*

POLLY: It's lonely in Mucka, isn't it, Miss Clem?

CLEMMY: It always was, Polly.

POLLY: Funny, I never noticed it before.

'POLLY'S SAD SONG'

POLLY: Oh! the plovers all call
          And the autumn leaves fall
          On the town in the turn of the year,
          As I sew a fine seam I sit and I dream
          For what has become of my dear?
EDIE, CLARRY & CLEMMY: Oh! What has become of her dear, oh dear,
          Oh, what has become of her dear?

          Will he ever come back
          Down the wallaby track
          With a song on his lips just for me?
          Or should I forget in the wild and the wet:
          Is my love just a fond memory?
EDIE, CLARRY & CLEMMY: Is her love just a fond memory, ee—ee,
          Her love just a fond memory?

CLEMMY: How well she remembers
          That burning December
          When he left on the train like a toff,
          As the train whistle blew, she suddenly knew
          Jack Tuesday was having it off.
EDIE, CLARRY & CLEMMY: Oh! Yes, he was having it off, off, off,
          Oh, yes he was having it off.

          POLLY *weeps.*

CLARRY: It was always her fate
          To be fatally late,
          And she knew he would never be true,
          But alack and a day she let him slip away,
          with a virginal flutter or two.
EDIE, CLARRY & CLEMMY: She'd a virginal flutter or two, oo—oo,
          a virginal flutter or two.

          POLLY *sobs louder.*

CLARRY & CLEMMY: And hour by hour
          Her heart's turning sour,
          While she sits here and sews a fine seam,
          She'll never get laid, she'll be just an old maid,

EDIE: With a hope chest that's full up with dreams.

ALL: Her/my hope chest is full up of dreams, it seems,
           Her/my hope chest is full up of dreams

> CECIL BRUNNER *has entered during the song, and now comes forward into the circle.*

CECIL: Good evening, ladies.

ALL: Good evening, Mr Brunner—I mean, Cecil.

CECIL: Quite a snap in the air this evening. Have an acid drop.

> *They all smile, incline their heads and take one.*

I hope I'm not intruding.

ALL: Oh! No, no, no!

CECIL: But I do have something of the utmost importance to say.

POLLY: I'm sure it must be very interesting.

CECIL: To Miss Polly.

EDIE: What's he saying?

CLARRY: [*shouting*] It's private.

EDIE: To who?

CLEMMY: Polly.

EDIE: Oh!

> *They all look at each other.* EDIE *rises.*

Miss Clemmy! Miss Clarry!

> *They both rise, smiling archly.*

CLARRY & CLEMMY: Good evening, Mr Brunner.

CECIL: [*embarrassed*] I don't mean to be precipitous.

CLARRY, CLEMMY & EDIE: Of course not, Mr Brunner.

> EDIE *farewells the* MISSES HUMMER *backstage, then crosses to* EEK *and shakes him.* POLLY *moves across to an old-style phonograph.*

POLLY: I'll just put a record on. It's the latest hit. They're dancing to it everywhere: Sydney, London, New York.

EEK: Secede, that's what we need—secession. I've said so for years. Wipe Canberra off the face of the earth, and go it alone.

> EDIE *keeps on shaking him.* EEK *takes off his headphones.*

Eh?

EDIE: Early night, Mr Perkins, dear.

EEK: But it's only just gone seven.

EDIE: Early to bed, early to rise, makes a man healthy, wealthy and wise.

> EDIE *makes faces at* EEK; *grumbling, he exits with her.* POLLY *has begun dancing around the room to the strains of 'You Made Me Love You', humming the tune.*

POLLY: Dance, Mr Brunner?

CECIL: These modern dances! I don't think… I know how.

POLLY: Of course you do. Look—it's easy. [*She demonstrates a few steps.*] Anyone can pick it up… in two ticks.

> CECIL *moves into* POLLY's *arms.*

Isn't it scrumptious?

CECIL: Oh! Miss Polly, if only we could go on dancing like this forever.

POLLY: You're pretty good really—for a beginner.

CECIL: [*archly*] You could give me dancing lessons.

POLLY: Would you like that?

CECIL: It would be… scrumptious.

POLLY: That's right. [*Laughing*] You're a card. I like a sense of humour.

> *She begins to sing the words of the song.*

> You made me love you,
> I didn't want to do it,
> I didn't want to do it,
> You made me love you…

CECIL: How appropriate!

POLLY: And all the time you knew it.…
> You made me happy,
> Sometime, you make me glad;
> But there were times, dear,
> When you made me feel so sad.

CECIL: Miss Polly… could we stop dancing now?

POLLY: Oh no, don't you love it?

CECIL: I can't talk and dance at the same time. It needs too much concentration.

> POLLY *whirls across and turns off the gramophone.*

POLLY: Well, and you were saying?

CECIL: Polly. You must know how I've been hoping—

POLLY: [*lightly*] While there's life there's hope—so they say.

CECIL: Hoping that… one of these days… you'd do me the honour of being my bride.

> POLLY *turns away. Enter* HARRY TUESDAY, *right, much the worse for wear. He sits under the monument with a bottle of beer.*

Oh, I know you were in love with Jack Tuesday, but he went away, under suspicious circumstances.

POLLY: He went away to be an actor.

CECIL: With two women in tow… [*Moving towards her*] My dear Polly, how could you ever take him back after that?

POLLY: No, of course I couldn't.

CECIL: No decent woman could.

POLLY: Of course not.

> *Pause.* CECIL *moves closer.*

CECIL: Marriage is a big step.

POLLY: There's not many eligible men in Mukinupin. No, let's face it, there aren't any eligible men in Mukinupin. I could hardly marry Harry Tuesday.

> *She giggles.*

CECIL: You probably don't think I'm eligible, either. But I love you, Polly, I always have, and I would make you a faithful husband.

POLLY: I know that… Cecil.

CECIL: And we could travel all round the country. It's an interesting life.

POLLY: Almost anything's better than Mukinupin.

CECIL: Then will you… marry me?

POLLY: I don't see why not.

CECIL: Does that mean yes?

POLLY: I suppose so.

> CECIL *takes* POLLY *in his arms. She is very unresponsive.*

CECIL: Oh! Polly, my dearest, you have made me the happiest man east of the rabbit-proof. Of course, I'll have to ask your father formally for your hand.

POLLY: Well then, let's get it over with. [*She goes upstage and calls off:*] Mother, Daddy, Mr Brunner—I mean Cecil—has got something to tell you!

Enter EDIE *and* EEK *looking self-conscious.*

They must have been listening outside the door.

Amused, she exits, tweaking EEK*'s ear. He looks pleased.*

EDIE: What was that, dear?

CECIL: Mr Perkins, may I have your permission to ask your daughter's hand in marriage?

EEK: Yes. But I don't like your chances.

CECIL: [*dignified*] She has already said yes.

EEK: Well! Did you hear that, Mother? I'll get out the cigars.

EDIE: Hear what?

EEK: Our Pol getting married to Cecil here.

EDIE bursts into tears and clasps CECIL to her.

EDIE: Oh! Mr Brunner—Cecil—you've made me the happiest of women.

EEK: Our Pol, grown and wed! It's hard for a man to lose his only daughter.

EDIE: But we're not losing a daughter—we're gaining a son.

Self-conscious laughter.

Give Cecil a glass of strawberry cordial, Father.

EEK: Got nothing stronger. I'm a wowser—and proud of it.

They all drink their cordial.

A toast—to Cecil and Polly.

EDIE: To Cecil and Polly. Have you decided on a long or a short engagement? I think a spring wedding's always appropriate, don't you? And it'd give her time to get her trousseau together. I'll just run across and tell Miss Hummer. She'll have to start in sewing right away. [*She stands dreaming in the doorway.*] I can see her now in white georgette embossed with lily of the valley, an ivory train caught by a coronet of pearls. We were married in the spring, weren't we, Eek? I was a city girl. I'd never seen the real country. At first we lived in that tin humpy at the back of the store, and I hung up all the family portraits, tinted to kill. They stared down at us, night and day; and sometimes I heard the dingoes howling from the salt lakes and the blacks... [*Shuddering*] The willy-willies blew the dust and the sheets of corrugated iron along the main street. Sometimes I thought, 'I'll die of the loneliness'—but, of course, I didn't. They were such long, hot summers; but I must have got used to them.

> EDIE *exits dreamily.* HARRY *sings drunkenly, unaccompanied.*

HARRY: New Holland is a barren place,
In it there grows no grain,
Nor any habitation
Wherein for to remain.

I'll plant her and I'll rape her,
I will not run her down,
Upon her gold and torment,
I'll build me shanty town.

CECIL: I think I ought to tell you, Mr Perkins—

EEK: Call me Eek.

CECIL: —that I do hope to keep Polly in the manner to which she's become accustomed.

EEK: Thank God we got rid of that young loafer, Jack Tuesday. Not the other one, though. He's still out there howling under the war memorial. National disgrace! We didn't put that up to be desecrated. Oh, I know they tell me he's a hero, but I can't stomach it. Feller like him, disgrace to the town, danger to the women folk.

> *They smoke their cigars and drink their cordial.*

It's queer though, Cec. As one white man to another, have you ever noticed? Women like a bastard, stirs something in them—maternal instinct. But I'm glad our Polly came to her senses. She was sweet on Jack Tuesday, no doubt about it, proves what I just said. They all love a swine. Come on, Cec lad, and we'll join the ladies.

> EEK *rises and moves front to stare up at the sky.*

Rain about. Just in time for the seeding.

CECIL: Good for the crops.

EEK: Superphosphate will save us all.

> *They exit back, chummily, as the sky darkens and the light*

changes towards an early rainy evening.

HARRY: [*singing*] She is my bitter heritage,
    She is my darling one,
    She drowns me in the winter
    And she breaks me in the sun

    TOUCH OF THE TAR *enters dressed in the bedraggled finery of her former appearance, barefoot and dirty, trailing her broken parasol. She moves centre stage uncertainly.*

TOUCH OF THE TAR: That you, 'Arry?

HARRY: [*very drunk*] No. Who's zat, eh, who's zat?

TOUCH OF THE TAR: It's me—Lily.

HARRY: Lily… Lily who?

TOUCH OF THE TAR: It's Lily Perkins.

HARRY: Oo! We've got tickets on ourselves, haven't we? Lily Perkins, eh? [*Laughing wildly, he rises and staggers over to her.*] Why, it's of Touch of the Tar 'erself. But what's all this, eh?! What's all this—flash clobber?

    He tears at her dress and it comes away in his hands.

TOUCH OF THE TAR: Me name's Lily Perkins.

    HARRY *begins to push her across the stage.*

Don' you touch me.

HARRY: Why?

TOUCH OF THE TAR: 'Cause you're an animal, thass why. You're a wild animal. Whadda you want, anyway? What you ever want from me? Same ting all the time, same ting.

HARRY: Your blood, that's what.

    More lightning flashes and thunder begins to roll.

TOUCH OF THE TAR: [*taunting him*] They reckon you're mad now, not right in the 'ead?

    HARRY *circles her dangerously.*

HARRY: Thass right.

TOUCH OF THE TAR: But you always was, I reckon, always was barmy, can't blame it on no war. Mad 'Arry Toosday.

HARRY: Stupid bitch! I'd like ter king-hit you with this bottle.

TOUCH OF THE TAR: Why doncha then, you dingo?

She skilfully dodges as he brings the bottle down on the ground, smashing it off for a weapon.

HARRY: What are y', eh? You're a harlot, that's what y' are. You never been faithful to me. Tell me, go'on. How many times?

He springs at her, knocks her down and raises the bottle over her head, kneeling over her.

Who'd you go with, eh? Who'd y' go with?

TOUCH OF THE TAR: Your bloody brother, that's who. I went with Jack.

She laughs wildly.

HARRY: I'll kill the dirty crawler. [*He raises the bottle but changes his mind.*] Ah, you're shit, you stink, you're not worth markin'. What can you expect from a gin, anyway? A man'd have to be mad.

He gets up and staggers away to the memorial.

TOUCH OF THE TAR: Me name's Lily, Lily Perkins.

HARRY: Nick orf.

TOUCH OF THE TAR: I reckon I don't like you, 'Arry... but I love you, by Jesus.

No answer.

Why didn't y' kill? I wanta die anyway. I come home ter die. [*Pause.*] But I ain't got no home.

There is a tapping of sticks, very softly. The bullroarer begins like an echo of itself, far away. TOUCH OF THE TAR *listens, humming to herself, tapping on the stage with her broken parasol.*

Rain's comin' up. I heard the black cockatoos fly over. Then we'll sleep in peace, we'll break the drought.

TOUCH OF THE TAR *sits cross-legged centre stage to the beating of sticks, the bull-roarer and the rolling thunder.*

You don't love me, 'Arry, an' I c'n do wivout you. I usta think I couldn't, that I'd die or somethink, but when the coppers come for you I never died, an' when you went to their bleedin' ol' war I never died neither, and 'ere I am still hangin' about on the edge of town...

She laughs wryly and begins to circle in a weird little dance, humming to herself, unfolding her broken parasol that hangs over her head like a parody. Her dance begins slowly, but gradually becomes wilder and wilder as the storm increases.

'TOUCH OF THE TAR'S SONG'

Lily Perkins is me name, the creek bed is me station,
It's no disgrace, 'cause me black face is the colour of the nation.
O boomerai an' mind her eye an' dance roun' in the bindi,
I got a boy in Mukerup an' one in Muckinbimbi.

Me daddy is as white as flour, me mam was black as coal,
An' then they comes, the Caflik nuns, an' taught me 'bout me soul.
I wish'd they'd left me in the creek where me ol' people dies,
The liddle child they found who cried, among the bindi-eyes.

I 'ad a liddle dream that I might catch a fallin' star,
But they took me down ter whitey town an' called me Touch o' Tar,
But when the wild duck cries at night it seems I gotta rise
With beatin' wings an' voice that sings out of the bindi-eyes.

The rain begins. She holds out her arms to it like a fertility rite, and puts up her ragged parasol. HARRY *hunches into a battered army greatcoat.*

It's rainin', 'Arry. The rain's come.

To the sound of rain and thunder she dances on.

Lily Perkins is me name, the creek bed is me station,
I am the spirit of the place, the colour of the nation.
Oh! boomerai an' mind yer eye an' don' kick up a shindy,
We'll all waltz in and out agen an' dance the wild corroboree.

During the song ZEEK *enters, dressed as before, with lantern, telescope, et cetera.*

ZEEK: 'Night, Lily. Creek's risin'.
TOUCH OF THE TAR: 'Night, ol' Zeek. You make rain wiv that thing?
ZEEK: Only God makes the rain.
TOUCH OF THE TAR: But nothin' for poor Lily, eh? [*She gives a sad*

little giggle as she moves off.] But never mind, 'Arry, we'll all die laughin', eh?

TOUCH OF THE TAR *exits.*

ZEEK: Feelin' bad, Harry?

HARRY: Pretty crook! The booze has got me, an' the gas… poison gas, y'know. [*Pause.*] There's a kind of bottomless horror, when the gruesome wind is blowin', and the ice is crackin' in the paddocks.

ZEEK: They reckon you won the Victoria Cross.

HARRY: Thass right.

ZEEK: What y' do with it?

HARRY: Give it ter Touch of the Tar for a fuck. [*He explodes into laughter.*] Nah, she wouldn't even take it, ignorant boong, I pawned it an' got shickered in Albany. I ain't never been back.

ZEEK *is peering through the telescope.*

ZEEK: There's somethin', out in that creek bed—and, by crikey, it's Touch of the Tar.

HARRY: Ah, she can swim like a blackfish. She couldn't drown if she wanted to.

ZEEK: She's got a rock tied round 'er middle. She'll drown alright.

HARRY: Silly bitch, we all gotta die. Why don't she just wait 'er turn? I'll die—like a dog in the scrub.

ZEEK: She's goin' down alright.

HARRY: It's bloody freezin' in there. I'm not goin' ter catch me death ter save 'er black hide.

ZEEK: And she ain't comin' up agen.

HARRY: Ah! Bugger 'er.

But he is galvanized into action and races off.

ZEEK: Water of life. Water of chaos. Water of destruction. The child in the womb is lapped with water, the pastures of the wilderness drip, the hills gird themselves with joy, the meadows clothe themselves with flocks, the valleys deck themselves with grain. We will irrigate the desert with the spring of living water, freshen the waters of the dead salt lake and make the well at the world's end swarm with fish…

HARRY *staggers on carrying the dripping* TOUCH OF THE TAR *in his arms. Thunder and lightning.*

HARRY: Give us a hand here, Zeek.

> ZEEK *hobbles across and together they bring* TOUCH OF THE TAR *around.*

She's comin' round.

ZEEK: Hey, Touch of the Tar!

HARRY: Don't call 'er that. She don't like it no more. She likes Lily. Pretty name, ain't it? Suits 'er too.

> TOUCH OF THE TAR *opens her eyes and smiles.*

TOUCH OF THE TAR: You still mad at me, 'Arry? [*Feebly she tries to sit up.*] It didn't work wiv Jack. Thass why I come back, okay?

HARRY: Okay!

TOUCH OF THE TAR: 'E said 'e was an outcast, but he weren't 'nough of an outcast for me.

> HARRY *pours some of the grog down her neck and she chokes and splutters.*

HARRY: There, get that inter y'. Better stuff than water.

> HARRY *cradles* TOUCH OF THE TAR *tenderly in his arms as* ZEEK *goes back to his telescope.*

TOUCH OF THE TAR: 'Arry, I got so tired.

HARRY: Of what?

TOUCH OF THE TAR: Of bein' the town slut, the town joke, the black velvet. You name it, I'm tired of it.

HARRY: We'll make it alright, Lil.

TOUCH OF THE TAR: [*happily*] You called me Lil.

HARRY: It's your name, ain't it?

TOUCH OF THE TAR: Do you love me, 'Arry?

HARRY: Die without y'. But I'm walkin' on ice with you, Lily. I always am.

> *She shivers.*

TOUCH OF THE TAR: Jeez, but I'm cold.

HARRY: Don't whinge. I can't stand a whinger.

> HARRY *crosses to* ZEEK'*s pack, takes a blanket and wraps her up carefully.*

TOUCH OF THE TAR: When you was away… in them trenches… I usta think, 'e's out there... in the dark... callin' to me... like me ol' people... wonderin' why I don't never come to 'im.

Thunder, lightning.

HARRY: They was all dead, every man Jack of 'em, lying out there in the moonlight, starin' up at the sky. I said, 'Mate, how about givin' us a hand here?' then, 'Hey! You bludgers, there's work ter be done', and then I knew, I was all on me Pat Malone.

TOUCH OF THE TAR: Will we get married, 'Arry?

HARRY: They called it No Man's Land.

TOUCH OF THE TAR: I believe in God, do you?

HARRY: Didn't use to, but I wanta be square now, Lily, an' do the straight by you. We'll leave this rotten town. We'll go across them salt lakes with the quail risin' up under our feet... Hey, Zeek, know anythin' about this marryin' business?

ZEEK: [*alarmed*] Marryin'? Me? No, I never been a marryin' man.

HARRY: Me neither, but now I'd like... a bit of a ceremony.

ZEEK scratches his head.

ZEEK: Eek's the lay preacher, but I was never much of a one for churches. Y'see I'm a religious man. [*He pauses, thinks.*] Hang on a minute. [*He rummages in his pack and pulls out a pocket Shakespeare.*] Just the ticket.

HARRY: What's that?

ZEEK: Will Shakespeare: merry, tragical, tedious and brief. [*He looks up towards the sky.*] Rain's easin', cloud's passin'. And now the moon like to a silver bow, new bent in heaven, shall behold the night of our solemnities. Go... bring the rabble.

Enter silently THE FLASHER, *who takes* ZEEK'*s hurricane lantern, lights it, and holds it up behind him.* ZEEK *rummages in his pack for a pair of battered glasses and places them solemnly on his nose.* HARRY *and* TOUCH OF THE TAR *kneel before* ZEEK. *There is the sound of a tapping stick and the weird night music begins, interrupted by the tapping sounds and the faint bullroarer.*

Highest Queen of State, Great Clemmy comes. I know her by her gait.

Enter CLEMMY. ZEEK *takes her arm.*

CLEMMY: Why has thou, Zeek, summoned me hither to this short grass'd green?
ZEEK: How does my bounteous sister?
Go with me
To bless this twain, that they may prosperous be,
And honour'd in their issue.
CLEMMY: This is a most majestic vision, and Harmonious charmingly.
HARRY: For Christ's sake, get on with it.
CLEMMY: Hush, and be mute,
Or else our spell is marr'd.
ZEEK: Look down ye gods,
And on this couple drop a blessed crown,
Quiet days, fair issue and long life.
Give me your hands, and by the merry rite of spring
I charge you lovers you are eternally knit.

> ZEEK *moves off to gaze in his telescope as* HARRY *and* TOUCH OF THE TAR *rise and embrace.* THE FLASHER *and* CLEMMY *form an arch of gum leaves.* HARRY *and* TOUCH OF THE TAR *move ceremoniously under the arch as* CLEMMY *and* THE FLASHER *sing.* TOUCH OF THE TAR *and* HARRY *move off into the distance like a mirage over the salt lakes.* ZEEK *has lost interest in the proceedings and is back amongst the stars.*

'THE MARRIAGE SONG'

CLEMMY: Honour, riches, marriage-blessing,
FLASHER: Long continuance and increasing,
ALL: Hourly joys be still upon you
As we sing our blessings on you.
Earth's increase and harvests plenty,
Barns and cradles never empty;
Vines with clustr'ing branches growing,
Wheat with goodly burden bowing.
Spring come to you from the farthest,
In the very end of harvest!
Scarcity and want shall shun you.
All our blessings now are on you.
Honour, riches, marriage-blessing.

ZEEK *jumps up and down in excitement.*

ZEEK: [*yelling*] By the jumping bleeding bloody Jesus, I've found another planet.

CLEMMY, *centre stage, gazes wistfully after* HARRY *and* TOUCH OF THE TAR. *She beats with her crutch on the stage.*

The stars are above, wherever we are. We walk the earth and gaze into eternity, we ride with Andromeda, see the holes in heaven...

FLASHER: And find the secret of perpetual motion.

Exit THE FLASHER *murmuring to his matchbox.*

Marconi the Great One, speak to me.

ZEEK *jumps up and down with excitement.*

ZEEK: [*yelling*] By the jumping bleeding bloody Jesus, I've found another planet!

Exit ZEEK *carrying the telescope.* CLEMMY *moves to her wicker chair and sits, hands folded. Lights up in the Perkins' parlour.* CLEMMY *rises and comes forward to greet* POLLY, *who enters in her wedding gown, carrying a portrait of* JACK, *followed by* CLARRY, *fixing her train, and* EDIE *fussing after her with the bridal bouquet.* POLLY *comes centre stage, looking melancholy and exasperated, tugging at her veil and displacing it as the two women fix it and* CLEMMY *tugs her dress here and there.*

'POLLY'S SAD WEDDING SONG'

POLLY: They dress me up in my wedding gown,
         But the love of my life is out of town,
         He's been out of town for many a day;
         Through autumn and winter and spring he's away,
         But the plover's song is still achingly sweet,
         Like a wave of shadow over the wheat.

Still holding the photograph, she climbs on the table with help from the women to have her hem adjusted in a similar scene to that in Act One.

         O Mother, dear Mother, I'm Queen of the May,
         You woke me up early on my wedding day,

But never again will I fall asleep,
To the song of the plover so achingly sweet,
So put on my veil and give me my ring,
And teach me the song it is proper to sing.

[*To the photo*] I've something borrowed and something blue,
But I haven't a thing that belongs to you;
Happy is the bride that the sun shines on,
Happy the crops that the rain rains on,
But I'd like to run on my leaden feet
Like a wave of shadow over the wheat.

They dress me up in my wedding gown,
But the love of my life is out of town,
He's been out of town for many a day;
Through autumn and winter and spring he's away,
But the plover's song is still achingly sweet,
Like a wave of shadow over the wheat.

EDIE *takes* JACK's *photograph from* POLLY *and tosses it away.*
POLLY *is helped down from the table and stands waiting.*
Enter EEK *dressed in clerical collar and good black suit. He*
gives POLLY *his arm and they move off in the direction of the*
Mukinupin Town Hall with EDIE *weeping and the two* MISSES
HUMMER *following.* CECIL BRUNNER *enters through the Town*
Hall archway and stands waiting, dressed in a morning suit.
POLLY *is crying quietly.*

ALL: [*except* POLLY] Don't be late for your wedding, dear Polly we
pray,
Polly we pray, Polly we pray,
If your bridegroom is jilted he'll cry lack-a-day,
Cry lack-a-day, cry lack-a-day,
Don't be late for your wedding, dear Pol.

As they reach the Mukinupin Town Hall, POLLY *turns front to dry*
her eyes. EEK, *very concerned, draws her aside.*

EEK: My darling child, are you sure you're happy?
POLLY: Of course I'm happy, Daddy. Can't you see—they're tears of
joy.

EEK: It's not too late to turn back.

POLLY: Too late, Daddy.

EEK: Better late than never. Oh, Pol, a loveless marriage is a sin against the spirit.

POLLY: Isn't it possible to make the best of it?

EEK: [*sadly*] It is possible.

POLLY: I'll do it, then. All girls cry on their wedding day.

> *She turns back and moves to* CECIL*'s side, smiling bravely.* EEK *leaves her side and, taking his prayer book from his pocket, mounts the steps in front of the Town Hall.*

EEK: Beloved brethren of Mukinupin, we are gathered together here in the sight of God and in the face of this congregation to join together this man and this woman in holy matrimony instituted of God in the time of Man's innocency.

> JACK TUESDAY *and* MERCY MONTEBELLO *have entered far right, carrying their ports, and both dressed in the height of fashion. Nobody notices them.*

It is not by any to be enterprised and taken in hand lightly, unadvisedly or wantonly, but reverently, discreetly, advisedly, soberly and in the fear of God. Therefore if any man can shew any just cause why ye may not be lawfully joined, let him now speak…

JACK: [*coming forward*] Yes, I can.

> *They all swing around.* POLLY *stares as if she had seen a ghost.*

EEK: [*faintly*]… or else hereafter hold his peace.

JACK: I can't hold my peace.

EEK, EDIE, CLARRY & CLEMMY: Why?

JACK: Because she doesn't love him.

EEK: Is that right, Polly?

POLLY: [*faintly*] Quite right, Father.

EEK: Then, why didn't you say so? It's too bad of you, Pol.

EDIE: [*angrily*] What's she say, what's she say?

CLARRY: [*shouting*] She won't marry Cecil!

EDIE: Oh, my God, my God, my smelling salts!

> *She goes to faint and is supported to a chair by the* MISSES HUMMER. EEK *goes to minister to her.* POLLY *turns to* CECIL.

POLLY: Mr Brunner—Cecil—I owe you an apology.

CECIL: It is a sad disappointment—Miss Polly.

POLLY: It's more than that. I've been cruel and dishonest and I should be punished for it, as I've no doubt I will be. Oh, Jack!

JACK moves forward and takes POLLY'*s hands.*

JACK: Marry me, Polly, that'll be punishment enough.

POLLY: But what about—Madame Montebello?

MERCY laughs lightly.

MERCY: Why, my dear—I'm old enough to be his ma.

POLLY: Yes, I know, but you're… so… beautiful.

MERCY: Thank you, I'm sure, but that doesn't alter the case.

POLLY: But I thought…

MERCY: A fertile imagination, Miss Polly, is no substitute for good sense.

CECIL: Hear, hear.

MERCY smiles at CECIL *and bows.*

POLLY: And Touch of the Tar…?

JACK: She ran away, back to Mukinupin, within a week.

MERCY: I'm afraid she just… didn't fit in. Oh, come, come, my dear, why don't you just take your Jack, and stop the cross-examinations.

JACK: Merc, you've hit the nail on the head as usual. But what about…?

MERCY: What about me? Why Jack—a comely woman can always fall on her feet, given the right set of circumstances.

CECIL: And they are, Madame?

MERCY: An eligible bachelor, and an eye for the main chance.

MERCY makes roguish eyes at CECIL *who is quite overcome.*

CECIL: Oh, Madame Montebello, if you could only take a broken heart…

MERCY: And make it whole? Why certainly, my dear, we could have a double wedding.

She moves into his arms.

CECIL: I could hardly hope for such happiness. Miss Polly…?

POLLY: I'm so happy for you, Cecil. So relieved for us all.

JACK: Me too. Put it there, Cec.

JACK *shakes* CECIL *violently by the hand.*

MERCY: So now, if we could perhaps rearrange ourselves.

POLLY *runs across to* EEK.

POLLY: Oh, Daddy, Daddy, I want to marry Jack, and Mercy wants to marry Cecil, so it's all turned out for the best after all.

CLARRY & CLEMMY: Oh! Polly, how marvellous!

EDIE: What's she say, what's she saying now?

CLARRY & CLEMMY: It's a double wedding, Mrs Perkins.

EDIE: Bigamy! Oh, my God… the smelling salts, the smelling salts?

EEK: Are you sure you've got it right this time, Polly?

POLLY: Oh! Daddy, yes, yes, absolutely scrumptiously sure.

EEK: What are your prospects, young man?

JACK: [*proudly*] I've got a contract with the Firm for three years at three quid a week in the second-back row of the chorus and, we're off to tour Maori Land in The Maid of the Mountains with Our Glad.

ALL: [*except* MERCY] Oh! Wonderful! What luck! Marvellous news, Jack! [*et cetera*]

JACK: And there'll be a place for Pol, too, she's got great legs and we know she can hit a high C. Oh, Pol, Pol, we can go anywhere from here. Ziegfeld is paying Evelyn Laye five thousand a week.

POLLY: Oh, Jack, you're such a marvel.

JACK: [*grinning*] Just a Mukinupin boy and proud of it.

MERCY: Jack will go far, I promise you. [*Hastily*] And Polly too, of course.

JACK: It's all settled, then.

JACK *and* POLLY *move off, arm in arm,* MERCY *and* CECIL *follow,* EEK *and* EDIE, *reconciled, follow and then the* MISSES HUMMER, *for 'The Wedding Dance'.*

'THE WEDDING DANCE'

JACK: Everything is turning up roses,
           Everything is turning out fine,
           Man proposes and God disposes
           To turn the water into wine.

           There's a definite silver lining,
           Blue skies don't turn to grey,

The sun will always come out shining
On a Mukinupin wedding day.

CECIL: Mercy Montebello, will you marry me?
MERCY: Why, Mr Brunner, certainement—ly.
JACK: Polly Perkins, will you be my wife,
To live together for the rest of my life?
POLLY: To live together in a dream of love,
JACK & POLLY: To kiss and cuddle like a turtle dove.
EDIE: Eek Perkins, will you give your daughter
To be his everloving bride?
EEK & EDIE: Through the storms of life and sunshine,
Walking gladly side by side,
ALL: [*chanting*] In sickness and health, for richer for poorer, for better
or worse,
To love and to cherish till death do us/them part.
EEK: Those whom God has joined together let no man put asunder.
ALL: Everything is turning up roses,
Everything is turning out fine,
Man proposes and God disposes
To turn the water into wine.

There's a definite silver lining,
Blue skies don't turn to grey,
The sun will always come out shining
On a Mukinupin wedding day.

POLLY *and* JACK *have danced over to the suitcases; the train
whistle is heard off. As* EDIE *and* EEK, CECIL *and* MERCY, *and
the two* MISSES HUMMER *wave, weep and throw kisses,* JACK *and*
POLLY *exit, carrying the luggage as the song dies away...*

POLLY & JACK: On a Mukinupin wedding day...
On a Mukinupin wedding day...
On a Mukinupin wedding day...
EEK: [*to EDIE*] Dry your eyes, Mother. It's time to open up Perkins'
General Store.
EDIE: Where's my Polly now?
EEK: Gone to make her fortune. She's a chip off the old block.

EEK *goes behind the counter and rings up his cash register.* EDIE *takes a feather duster and begins dusting the shop, and anything else within sight. The light begins to fail.*

EDIE: [*sniffing*] Life is real! Life is earnest!
And the grave is not the goal;
'Dust thou art to dust returnest',
Was not spoken of the soul.

Lives of great men all remind us
We can make our lives sublime,
And, departing, leave behind us
Footprints on the sands of time.

CLARRY *takes up the shop broom and begins to purposefully sweep the stage.* CLEMMY *hobbles to her wicker chair and fans herself with her sandalwood fan.* CECIL *strolls across, arm in arm with* MERCY.

EEK: I suppose you'll be off on the road again soon, Brunner?
MERCY: Certainly not. Cecil and I are opening up the best fish and chip shop in Mukinupin.
CECIL: Have another acid drop, my precious.
MERCY: Certainement, my love.

MERCY *and* CECIL *promenade, arm in arm, backstage to the scrim and stand as if posed forever in a photograph album.* EEK *rings up his last change in the till, and follows them to the scrim.*

EEK: Coming, Mother?
EDIE: I won't be long, Mr Perkins.

EDIE *hobbles out front, shading her eyes.*

[*Reciting again*] Art is long, and Time is fleeting,
And our hearts, though stout and brave,
Still like muffled drums, are beating
Funeral marches to the grave.

She moves backstage, and she and EEK *pose for their eternal photographs against the scrim.*

CLARRY: [*briskly*] Time to go, Clemmy. I've locked all the doors, swept the stage and blessed the place.

CLEMMY *rises painfully to her feet.*

Take my arm, dear, and we'll… whirl off into the dark.

The weird night music begins on the soundtrack very faintly, as they move off.

What about Polly and Jack?

CLEMMY: Oh, they'll never come back. They're playing Chu Chin Chow with Oscar Ashe and the camels.

CLARRY: And Harry and Touch of the Tar have gone bush over the salt lakes. Do you think they've found Paradise?

CLEMMY: Paradise is mighty hard to find.

CLARRY: Like Zeek Perkins fishing in the dust all the days of his life.

CLEMMY: He never found fresh water in Mukinupin.

The night music grows in volume as CLARRY *and* CLEMMY *take their immortal places before the scrim. Silence. A pause, then* THE FLASHER *gives one of his unearthly screams from the creek bed.*

MERCY: And now the Mukinupin Glee Club of the Ladies' Auxiliary of the RSL presents…

A drum roll as MERCY *turns and gives it all she's got…*

'THE MUKINUPIN CAROUSEL'

MERCY *bows and they all sweep into the final song and dance routine. The dance should be circular and reconciliatory in mood.*

ALL: Take a whirl on a carousel,
        Into the dark on a carousel,
        Deserts and stars have served us well,
        So let's all ride on a carousel.

MERCY & CECIL: Skeletons, acid drops, tea in china,
        Dry the dishes, what could be finer,
        Counting the sheep going into the pen,
        Counting them over and over again.

EEK & EDIE: Fire and blood and sand and water,
        The church bells toll for the storekeeper's daughter,
        Birth and magic and moth and rust,
        Close the curtain because we must.

CLARRY & CLEMMY: Love-in-the-mist and salvation jane,

Down in the creek bed praying for rain,
Ring a roses and round we go,
Close the curtain and end the show.

ALL: Take a whirl on a carousel,
Into the dark on a carousel,
Desert and stars have served us well,
So let's all ride on a carousel.

The music plays faster and faster as they whirl into a total blackout, and darkness falls on Mukinupin.

THE END

NOTES

The Man from Mukinupin makes many references to popular and classical works familiar to the reader, particularly Shakespere. Besides the Montebellos' travesty, 'The Strangling of Desdemona', the reader will have recognised Lady Macbeth behind Edie's sleep-walking scene and the marriage ceremony of Miranda and Ferdinand from *The Tempest* in the 'wedding' of Lily and Harry. Quotations from *A Midsummer Night's Dream* are also found, particularly in Zeek's speeches. Below are the sources of other quotations and pastiches which may be less easily identifiable.

p.4, ls.9–10: Robert Browning, 'How They Brought the Good News from Ghent to Aix'.

p.10, ls.28–33: Alfred Lord Tennyson, 'Lilian'.

p.14, ls.6–7: Henry Lawson, 'The Roaring Days'.

pp.21–22: 'An 'Am, an Egg and an Onion', traditional song.

p.26, ls.16–23: Thomas Babington Macaulay, 'Horatius', in *Lays of Ancient Rome*.

p.32, ls.24–25: A traditional West Australian anthem. The author is unknown.

p.32, ls.31–32: After Tennyson.

p.37, ls.18–21: An old English fertility chant, quoted in Richard Cavendish (ed.), *Man, Myth and Magic*, New York, 1970.

pp.38–39: 'Harry Tuesday's Song' owes something to the traditional folk song 'Jim Jones'.

p.44, ls.9–12: Mary Gilmore, 'The Aboriginals'.

pp.46–47: For the first verse and the thought behind 'The New Holland Song' the author is indebted to Randolph Stow's character, Byrnie, in his novel *Tourmaline* (London, 1963). The last lines of *Tourmaline* read: 'Beware my testament! (Ah, my New Holland; my gold, my darling.) I say we have a bitter heritage. That is not to run it down.'

p.50, ls.4–10 Will Ogilvie, 'The Australian'.

pp.54–55: 'Flash Jack of Mukinupin', a parody of the traditional folk song 'Flash Jack from Gundagai'.

p.69, 1s.31–34 & p.70, ls 4–7: A traditional Diggers' song from the Great War.

p.79: 'Touch of the Tar's Song' owes something to the traditional folk song 'Old Black Alice'.

p.90, 1s.3–10, 26–29: Henry Wadsworth Longfellow, 'A Psalm of Life'.

Dorothy Hewett achieved distinction as a playwright, poet and novelist. Her stage works include *The Chapel Perilous, Mrs Porter and the Angels, Bon-Bons and Roses for Dolly, The Golden Oldies, Pandora's Cross, The Man from Mukinupin, Golden Valley, The Fields of Heaven* and *Nowhere*. The plays range in style but all exploit the imaginative possibilities of language, music and theatrical effects. Many of her early plays in particular shocked audiences with their explicit female sexuality, and she retained a maverick image and an ability to polarise audiences and critics through her life. Hewett also published eleven volumes of poetry, with three novels, a collection of short stories and an autobiography.

www.ingramcontent.com/pod-product-compliance
Lightning Source LLC
Chambersburg PA
CBHW041931090426
42744CB00017B/2012